TEST YOUR GRAMMAR

5

Kunze / Woxbrandt / Rowden

TEST YOUR GRAMMAR 5 • Adjectives & Adverbs
Lern- und Übungsgrammatik mit integriertem Key
Erarbeitet von: Claus Kunze, Barbro Woxbrandt, Lorna Rowden
ISBN 3-926686-39-1

THE TEST YOUR GRAMMAR SERIES

TEST YOUR GRAMMAR 1 • Nouns
ISBN 3-926686-35-9

TEST YOUR GRAMMAR 2 • Pronouns
ISBN 3-926686-36-7

TEST YOUR GRAMMAR 3 • Verbs
ISBN 3-926686-37-5

TEST YOUR GRAMMAR 4 • Participles, Gerund, Infinitive
ISBN 3-926686-38-3

TEST YOUR GRAMMAR 5 • Adjectives & Adverbs
ISBN 3-926686-39-1

© **Beaver Books**   C. Kunze / B. Woxbrandt   2005

Alle Rechte vorbehalten. Das Werk und alle seine Teile sind urheberrechtlich geschützt. Jede Verwertung in anderen als den gesetzlich zugelassenen Fällen bedarf der vorherigen schriftlichen Genehmigung des Verlages.

All rights reserved. No part of this publication may be reproduced or utilized, in any forms or by any means, without the prior permission of the copyright holders and publishers.

KATALOGE, INFORMATION & DIREKTBESTELLUNGEN BEI

BEAVER BOOKS • Marburger Str. 15 • 60487 Frankfurt
Tel. 069 – 77 40 47 • Fax 70 46 35
www.beaverbooks.de • e-mail: info@beaverbooks.de

GRAMMATIK: DES LEBENS GOLDENER BAUM

„Grau ist alle Theorie, und grün des Lebens goldener Baum." – Das ist zwar von Goethe und stimmt auch oft, aber man irrt, wenn man daraus den Schluss zieht, man könne die „graue" Grammatiktheorie links liegen lassen, damit der Sprachbaum um so schneller wachse. Ohne Wurzeln, Stamm und Zweige gibt es keinen Baum und ohne strukturierende Grammatik keine sprachliche Kommunikation. Kennt man die Regeln der Fremdsprache nicht, fällt man automatisch auf die der eigenen Muttersprache zurück. Das Resultat sind dann allerdings meist keine goldenen Bäume, sondern windschiefe Verwachsungen und unverständliches Wortgestrüpp.

TEST YOUR GRAMMAR soll nicht nur vor solchen Fehlleistungen bewahren, vor allen Dingen werden Sie sehen: Grammatik ist selber schon des Lebens goldener Baum. Jede gelernte Struktur begrünt sich sogleich mit frischen Wortschatzknospen und treffenden idiomatischen Wendungen und wächst so zu umgangssprachlich und situativ korrektem Englisch, das Sie in einer Vielzahl von klar aufgebauten und unterhaltsamen Tests trainieren und verfestigen können.

Erleben Sie also Ihren persönlichen Grammatikfrühling: Erwecken Sie vergessen geglaubte Kenntnisse aus dem Winterschlaf oder bringen Sie vorhandene Fähigkeiten zur Blüte – und pflanzen Sie gerne auch ein paar neue Bäumchen.

TEST YOUR GRAMMAR 5 • ADJECTIVES & ADVERBS

'A full-flavoured, medium-bodied, everyday-affordable wine' (wine guide), *'a tightly-curled, skull-hugging, poodle-cut hairdo'* (Anne Tyler), *'Austrian-born, once-scrawny muscle-man-turned-action-movie-hero Arnold Schwarzenegger'* (Time) – Das Englische scheint von Adjektiven gar nicht genug bekommen zu können, wobei es sich aus einem schier unerschöpflichen germanisch-romanischen Wortschatzerbe bedienen kann. Dazu kommt die enorme Flexibilität bei der Bildung zusammengesetzter Adjektive und bei der Ableitung aus anderen Wortklassen, von der die Sprache mit immer wieder treffenden und originellen Neuschöpfungen regen und phantasievollen Gebrauch macht. Die Welt der englischen Adjektive wird so zu einem stets blühenden Garten, in den wir Sie herzlich einladen möchten.

Adverbien: Inhaltlich ist es nur ein kleiner Schritt vom Adjektiv zum Adverb: Bezieht sich das Adjektiv auf eine Person oder Sache – *Liz is beautiful* – beschreibt das Adverb eine Handlung: *Liz sings beautifully*, oder ein Adjektiv: *The table was beautifully decorated*, oder einen ganzen Satzinhalt: *Surprisingly, none of us had heard of George's illness*.

Da im Deutschen Adjektive und Adverbien die gleiche Form haben, ist das Vergessen des *-ly* eine typische Schwierigkeit deutscher Muttersprachler, auf die sich die Regeln und Tests deshalb besonders konzentrieren.

Andererseits behalten nicht wenige Adverbien die Adjektivform (ohne '-ly') bei: *Take it easy; Don't drive so fast.* – Vorsicht ist auch bei bestimmten Verben geboten, die auf Zustände oder Eigenschaften des Subjekts oder Objekts verweisen. Diese werden mit einem Adjektiv verbunden: *You look great. – I feel tired.*

Und jetzt: *Work hard. Fill in the tests correctly. Thoroughly enjoy yourself.*

HINWEIS

Zur Verdeutlichung von „typisch deutschen" Fehlern werden auch sprachlich falsche Formulierungen aufgeführt; diese sind *kursiv* gesetzt und in *grauen Buchstaben* gehalten und werden durch ein vorangestelltes * gekennzeichnet, z. B.

I go often to the cinema.* – **Richtig: I **often go** to the cinema.

CONTENTS

ADJEKTIVE

Übersicht	9	
Die Steigerung der Adjektive • Übersicht	10	
Die Steigerung der Adjektive	11	TEST 1

BILDUNG VON ADJEKTIVEN AUS SUBSTANTIVEN UND VERBEN

Substantiv → Adjektiv	12	TEST 2
Evolutionary progress • Substantiv → Adjektiv	13	TEST 3
We are not amused • Verb → Adjektiv: Participles	14	TEST 4
Verb → Adjektiv: Participles	15	TEST 5

A narrow mind and a wide mouth . . .   *. . . usually go together.*
Hillary Clinton

WIT & WISDOM

Adjektive in Aphorismen	16	TEST 6
Office Wisdom • Adjektive in Aphorismen	17	TEST 7

COMPOUND ADJECTIVES • ZUSAMMENGESETZTE ADJEKTIVE

Bright-eyed and bushy-tailed • Adjective + (Noun+-ed) = Adjective	18	TEST 8
Complete the Sentences	19	TEST 9
High-minded and far-sighted • Adjective + (Noun+-ed)=Adjective	20	TEST 10
Quick-witted Synonyms • Low-spirited = sad	21	TEST 11
Be grammar-conscious • Noun + Adjective = Adjective	22	TEST 12
A breathtaking exercise • Noun + (Verb+ing) = Adjective	23	TEST 13
Action-packed & tailor-made • Noun + Past Participle = Adjective	24	TEST 14
Complete the Sentences	25	TEST 15
The big-prize test • Adjective + Noun = Adjective	26	TEST 16
A first-class high-speed test • Adjective + Noun = Adjective	27	TEST 17
Up-to-date information • Zusammensetzungen als Adjektiv	28	TEST 18
A state-of-the-art test • Wortzusammensetzungen als Adjektiv	29	TEST 19

CONTENTS

ADJEKTIVE & NOUN PARTNERSHIPS · COLLOCATION

Cool Collocations • Adjective & Noun Partnerships	30	TEST 20
Adjective & Noun Partnerships	31	TEST 21
Choose the correct Adjective • Multiple Choice • 1	32	TEST 22
Choose the correct Adjective • Multiple Choice • 2	33	TEST 23
Collocation Trios • 1	34	TEST 24
Collocation Trios • 2	35	TEST 25

ADJEKTIVE & NOUN PARTNERSHIPS · FIXED PAIRS

Find the happy medium • Fixed Pairs	36	TEST 26
Deutsch: Nominalkonstruktion → Englisch: Adjektiv + Substantiv	37	TEST 27
With flying colours • -ing-Partizip + Substantiv • Fixed Pairs	38	TEST 28
Living proof • -ing-Partizip + Substantiv • Fixed Pairs	39	TEST 29
Mixed bag • Past Participle + Substantiv • Fixed Pairs	40	TEST 30
Make a concentrated effort • Past Participle + Substantiv	41	TEST 31

SYNONYMS & ANTONYMS

Adjektiv-Synonyme	42	TEST 32
Cool, calm & collected • Adjektiv-Synonyme	43	TEST 33
Odd one out • Adjektiv-Synonyme	44	TEST 34
A pleasant / agreeable Test	45	TEST 35
Dead or alive • Adjektiv - Antonyme	46	TEST 36
More Antonyms	47	TEST 37
Find the Antonym Pairs	48	TEST 38
Find two Antonyms	49	TEST 39

*We, the willing,
following the unknowing
and the ungrateful,
are doing the impossible.*

ADJEKTIVE ALS SUBSTANTIVE

A test for the intelligent • Substantivierte Adjektive	50	TEST 40
May the best person win • Einzelpersonen und Einzeldinge	51	TEST 41

ADVERBEN

Übersicht	52	
Bildung der Adverben mit -ly • Übersicht	53	
Analyse this test closely • Verb + Adverb Kombinationen	54	TEST 42
Verb & Adverb Partnerships	55	TEST 43
For highly intelligent people only • Adverb + Adjective Partnerships	56	TEST 44
Clearly visible Word Partnerships: Adverb + Adjective	57	TEST 45
Absolutely correct • More Adverb + Adjective Partnerships	58	TEST 46
Deutsch-Englische Adverb + Adjektiv-Kombinationen	59	TEST 47
Adjective or Adverb? • Complete the sentences	60	TEST 48
Frequently asked questions • Adverb + Adjective + Noun	62	TEST 49
Sentence Adverbs • Satzadverben	63	TEST 50
A careful driver drives carefully • Rewrite the Sentences	64	TEST 51
Revision • Translate	65	TEST 52
Think big! • Adjektiv und Adverb gleiche Form	66	TEST 53
Looking good! • Linking Verbs	68	TEST 54
Sounds great! • Linking Verbs	69	TEST 55
Stellung der Adverbien im Satz • Übersicht	70	
Korrekte Position der Adverbien im Satz	71	TEST 56
Translate	71	TEST 57

KEY

Lösungen zu allen Tests	73	

INFO BOXES • ZUSATZINFORMATIONEN IM KEY

Word List: Adjektiv + (Substantiv + -ed) = Adjektiv	76	INFO 1
Word List: Substantiv + Present Participle (-ing) = Adjektiv	77	INFO 2
Word List: Substantiv + Past Participle (-ed/3.Form) = Adjektiv	78	INFO 3
Word List: Adjektiv + Substantiv = Adjektiv	79	INFO 4
Word List: Complex Adjectives	80	INFO 5
Collocation: Word Partnerships	81	INFO 6
Collocation: Fixed Pairs	83	INFO 7
Deutsch: Nominalzusammensetzung – Englisch: Adjektiv + Substantiv	83	INFO 8
Adjektive als Substantive	88	INFO 9
Satzadverbien als Kurzantwort	91	INFO 10

ADJECTIVES

a long-legged animal

smart - stylish - fashionable

a royal palace

musical instruments

a tall / **Nicht:** *high* building

a splitting headache

shark-infested waters

a gift-wrapped present

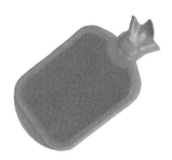
a hot-water bottle

ADJECTIVES

ADJEKTIVE

Adjektive beschreiben die Eigenschaften und Merkmale von Personen, Sachen oder Begriffen. Die meisten Adjektive können sowohl attributiv (vor einem Substantiv stehend) wie prädikativ (als Ergänzung auf bestimmte Verben folgend) verwendet werden.

Attributiver Gebrauch: an interesting story · a nice boy · the red car
Prädikativer Gebrauch: The story was interesting. · Laura looks nice. · This sounds great.

1. Die meisten Adjektive können gesteigert werden ▶ TEST 1

   a. Steigerung mit -er und -est: high – higher – highest

   b. Steigerung mit more und most: expensive – more expensive – most expensive

2. Viele Adjektive werden aus anderen Wortarten abgeleitet

   Substantiv → Adjektiv post → postal · luck → lucky · fear → fearful ▶ TESTS 2 & 3

   Verb → Adjektiv amuse → amusing · annoy → annoyed ▶ TESTS 4 & 5

3. Das Englische ist reich an zusammengesetzten Adjektiven, die bestimmten Mustern folgen

Adjektiv + (Substantiv + -ed) grey-haired · short-sighted · bright-eyed ▶ TESTS 8 – 11

Substantiv + Adjektiv bullet-proof vest · lead-free petrol ▶ TEST 12

Substantiv + (Verb + -ing) English-speaking · breathtaking · labour-saving ▶ TEST 13

Substantiv + (-ed/3.Form) action-packed · state-owned · air-conditioned ▶ TESTS 14 & 15

Adjektiv + Substantiv fast-track (career) · open-air (concert) ▶ TESTS 16 & 17

Complex Adjectives all-you-can-eat buffet · stop-and-go traffic ▶ TESTS 18 & 19

4. Bestimmte Adjektive treten in typischen „Partnerschaften" mit bestimmten Substantiven auf

pouring rain · bright light · accurate description · short break ▶ TESTS 20 – 25

Viele Adjektive sind mit bestimmten Substantiven so fest verwachsen, dass sie als 'Fixed Pairs' eine Sinneinheit bilden und als eigenständiger Eintrag in Wörterbüchern zu finden sind.

political party · chemical engineer · mashed potatoes · British Isles ▶ TESTS 26 – 31

5. Synonyme und Antonyme

Synonyme: Worte gleicher oder ähnlicher Bedeutung: clever – intelligent ▶ TESTS 32 – 35

Antonyme: Worte von entgegengesetzter Bedeutung: happy – sad ▶ TESTS 36 – 39

Es ist sinnvoll, sich zu allen Adjektiven stets auch die dazugehörigen Synonyme und Antonyme einzuprägen.

6. Substantivierte Adjektive

Einige Adjektive können auch als Substantive verwendet werden:

We must help the poor. · Always expect the unexpected. ▶ TESTS 40 & 41

ADJECTIVES

DIE STEIGERUNG DER ADJEKTIVE

REGELMÄSSIGE STEIGERUNG MIT – ER / – EST

Einsilbige Adjektive & zweisilbige Adjektive auf -ow, -er, -le, -y

old → older → oldest • weak → weaker → weakest • slow → slower → slowest
narrow → narrower → narrowest • gentle → gentler → gentlest • happy → happier → happiest

Ein stummes -e am Ende entfällt

nice → nicer → nicest • large → larger → largest • safe → safer → safest
wide → wider → widest

Endkonsonanten nach Einzelvokalen werden in einsilbigen Wörtern verdoppelt

mad → madder → maddest • big → bigger → biggest • slim → slimmer → slimmest
thin → thinner → thinnest • hip → hipper → hippest • fat → fatter → fattest

Der Endbuchstabe -y nach Konsonant wird zu -i

early → earlier → earliest • dirty → dirtier → dirtiest • dry → drier → driest
friendly → friendlier → friendliest • angry → angrier → angriest
Ausnahmen: shy → shyer → shyest • sly → slyer → slyest

STEIGERUNG MIT MORE / MOST: ADJEKTIVE MIT ZWEI UND MEHR SILBEN

rapid → more rapid → most rapid   famous → more famous → most famous
honest → more honest → most honest   careful → more careful → most careful

UNREGELMÄSSIGE STEIGERUNG

good → better → best • bad → worse → worst • much → more → most • little → less → least

---

FERNER IST ZU BEACHTEN

Einige zweisilbige Adjektive können nach beiden Arten gesteigert werden.

I've never met a **politer** person than Ian.   I've never met a **more polite** person than Ian.
Sue is **cleverer** than Michael.   Sue is **more clever** than Michael.
John is the **gentlest** man I know.   John is the **most gentle** man I know.

Zusammengesetzte Adjektive werden meist mit *more* und *most* gesteigert.

cold-blooded → more cold-blooded → most cold-blooded
hard-nosed → more hard-nosed → most hard-nosed

Bei einigen solcher Zusammensetzungen kann aber auch das Adjektiv (oder Adverb) gesteigert werden.

low-paid → lower-paid → lowest-paid • short-lived → shorter-lived → shortest-lived
long-lasting → longer-lasting → longest-lasting • nice-looking → nicer-looking → nicest-looking
good-looking → better-looking → best-looking • well-paid → better-paid → best-paid
badly-planned → worse-planned → worst-planned

Test 1

large — larger — largest

STEIGERN SIE DIE FOLGENDEN ADJEKTIVE

awful	**more awful**	**most awful**	hot		
busy	**busier**	**busiest**	impolite		
cheap			intelligent		
comfortable			many		
deep			narrow		
distant			pretty		
dull			quick		
expensive			quiet		
extreme			sad		
famous			silly		
fine			simple		
free			solid		
funny			strong		
heavy			terrible		

WORD FORMATION

Test 2

SUBSTANTIV → ADJEKTIV

Viele Adjektive werden durch Anhängen einer Nachsilbe (Suffix) aus Substantiven abgeleitet.

Da der Bereich der Wortbildung sehr komplex ist, können hier nur einige grundlegende Beispiele gegeben werden. Bitte beachten Sie auch die verschiedenen Endungsvarianten.

	SUBSTANTIV → ADJEKTIV		
-al	nation → national	culture → cultural	industry → industrial
-ary	evolution → evolutionary	diet → dietary	
-ful	event → eventful	grace → graceful	beauty → beautiful
-less	dream → dreamless	grace → graceless	fault → faultless
-ly	friend → friendly	day → daily	night → nightly
-ous	fame → famous	virtue → virtuous	fury → furious · disaster → disastrous
-y	dust → dusty	wit → witty	bone → bony · star → starry

A blood __bloody__   B envy _____   C order _____

   brother _____   force _____   parliament _____

   centre _____   form _____   poison _____

   change _____   frost _____   profession _____

   cost _____   function _____   rain _____

   coward _____   ghost _____   respect _____

   cream _____   glory _____   revolution _____

   dirt _____   legend _____   rock _____

   education _____   luck _____   ruin _____

   element _____   moment _____   scandal _____

   emotion _____   neighbour _____   sun _____

   end _____   night _____   year _____

Test 3

EVOLUTIONARY PROGRESS

Leiten Sie Adjektive aus den Substantiven der grauen Box ab und vervollständigen Sie die Ausdrücke.

A	o child	o environment	o globe	o power	o region
B	o music	o sand	o stress	o tact	o week
C	o class	o dream	o **evolution**	o force	o harmony
D	o clinic	o limit	o mystery	o sense	o tradition

A _____ accent

_____ couple

_____ economy

_____ engine

_____ disaster

B _____ beach

_____ diplomat

_____ instrument

_____ job

_____ magazine

C _____ personality

_____**evolutionary**_____ progress

_____ relationship

_____ sleep

_____ society

D _____ stranger

_____ supply

_____ tests

_____ values

_____ violence

WORD FORMATION

Test 4

WE ARE NOT AMUSED

'We are not amused' soll Königin Victoria gesagt haben,
als ein Diener eine Hofdame imitierte; mit anderen Worten: er war nicht **amusing**.
Partizipien wie **amusing** und **amused** sind Verbformen, die als Adjektive verwendet werden können.
PRESENT PARTICIPLE (Infinitiv + -ing) hat aktivische Grundbedeutung – *an amusing story*.
PAST PARTICIPLE (-ed/3. Form) hat passivische Grundbedeutung – *an amused listener*.

Bilden Sie die zu den Definitionen passenden Partizipien (A: Present Participles; B: Past Participles)

A	**alarm**	challenge	convince	distract	overwhelm	threaten	welcome
B	**amuse**	annoy	inspire	please	refresh	tempt	terrify

A 1. Something which causes you to be worried or concerned is _____**alarming**_____

2. An argument that makes you believe that sth is true, real or correct is _____

3. Someone who is friendly when you arrive is _____

4. An amount which is vast, much greater than other amounts is _____

5. Something that seems likely to cause harm is _____

6. Something which is demanding and difficult in a stimulating way is _____

7. Something that makes you unable to concentrate properly is _____

B 8. If you find something funny you're _____**amused**_____

9. If you're upset or angry about something you're _____

10. If something makes you feel cool or energetic again you're _____

11. When you'd like to do something (which maybe you shouldn't) you're _____

12. If something makes you feel enthusiastic and interested you're _____

13. If you feel very frightened you're _____

14. If you're delighted or happy about something you're _____

Test 5

Liz: That man over there is really _____ (annoy).
Sue: But he's not even looking at you.
Liz: I know, that's why I'm so _____ (annoy).

VERVOLLSTÄNDIGEN SIE DIE SÄTZE MIT DEN PASSENDEN ADJEKTIV-PARTIZIPIEN

A 1. The world's number of tropical rain forests is shrinking at an _____**alarming**_____ rate.

2. Martha was extremely ambitious and she soon got a _____ job in the City.

3. I don't find these arguments very _____ , they don't really prove anything.

4. I can't concentrate on my work when the radio is on, I find that very _____ .

5. Penny opened the door and gave Ken a warm _____ smile. He immediately felt at home.

6. It was a landslide victory for Labour, they won with an _____ majority.

7. The _____ behaviour of some aggressive hooligans really frightened us.

B 8. Our daughter loves our dog and playing with him can keep her _____**amused**_____ for hours.

9. After a fortnight in a luxurious spa hotel Joan felt energetic and _____ again.

10. My sister was _____ of walking home in the dark after seeing the horror film.

11. I felt _____ to have a piece of chocolate cake until my wife reminded me of my diet.

12. Many artists are _____ by the beauty of nature.

13. Our parents were very _____ when my sister told them she'd won the school prize.

14. The passengers were very _____ when the airline announced a delay.

15

ADJECTIVES

Test 6

Men marry because they are tired, women because they are curious. Both are disappointed.

WIT & WISDOM

Vervollständigen Sie die Aphorismen mit den passenden Adjektiven.

A	content	lonely	right	useless	**wise**	wonderful
B	brave	narrow	old	poor	smart	successful

A

1. He who thinks himself _____**wise**_____, oh heavens, is a great fool. (Voltaire)

2. How _____ is that flash of a moment when we realize we have discovered a friend.

3. War does not determine who is _____ – only who is left. (Bertrand Russell)

4. Nothing makes us so _____ as our secrets. (Paul Tournier)

5. To be _____ with little is difficult, to be _____ with much is impossible.

6. No man is _____ in this world who lightens the burden of someone else. (C. Dickens)

B

7. Anyone can get _____, all you have to do is live long enough.

8. A _____ mind and a wide mouth usually go together.

9. We might all be _____, if we followed the advice we give to our friends.

10. Fifty-one per cent of being _____ is knowing what you are dumb about. (Ann Landers)

11. You can't be _____, if you only have wonderful things happen to you.

12. If a society can't help the many who are _____, it can't save the few who are rich. (J.F. Kennedy)

Test 7

A clean desk is a sign . . . . . . of a cluttered desk drawer.

ALEC SMART — OFFICE WISDOM

OFFICE WISDOM

Vervollständigen Sie die Aphorismen mit den passenden Adjektiven.

A	busy	cheap	**confused**	happy	mediocre	young
B	empty	honest	idiot-proof	open	right	unnecessary

A
1. If you're not _____**confused**_____, you're not paying attention.
2. Only a _____ person is always at his best. (Somerset Maugham)
3. No one is too _____ to talk about how _____ he is.
4. Talk is _____ – until you hire a lawyer.
5. You're only _____ once, but you can be immature forever.
6. If ignorance is bliss, why aren't there more _____ people?

B
7. When two men in business always agree, one of them is _____ .
8. What is worse: talking when one's mouth is full or talking when one's head is _____ ?
9. You may be on the _____ track, but if you just sit there you'll get run over.
10. _____ confession is good for the soul, but bad for your career.
11. Minds are like parachutes—they only work when they are _____ .
12. Make something _____ and someone makes a better idiot.

COMPOUND ADJECTIVES

Test 8

As you know, we'll be cleaning up the forest tomorrow, so I want you all up early – bright-eyed and bushy-tailed!

BE BRIGHT-EYED and BUSHY-TAILED

Das Englische kennt eine Vielzahl von Adjektiven nach dem Muster: Adjektiv + (Substantiv+-ed).
Sie dienen der lebendigen und einprägsamen Beschreibung von Menschen und Dingen.

a black-haired man = a man with black hair
a long-legged actress = an actress with long legs

Führen Sie die Adjektive mit den passenden Substantiven zusammen.

	A			C	
full-bodied	**wine**	businessman	fast-paced		idealist
hard-nosed		story	full-throated		thriller
long-winded		determination	high-minded		support
single-minded	**wine**		whole-hearted		laugh

	B			D	
deep-rooted		hooligan	far-sighted		car
foul-mouthed		prejudices	high-powered		view
high-heeled		comedy	one-sided		shirt
light-hearted		shoes	short-sleeved		strategy

18

Test 9

a long-haired rock star

a double-breasted jacket

a broad-shouldered bodybuilder

VERVOLLSTÄNDIGEN SIE DIE SÄTZE MIT DEN AUSDRÜCKEN DER GEGENÜBERLIEGENDEN SEITE

A – B 1. The waiter recommended a ____**full-bodied wine**____ to go with our pasta dishes.

2. After-dinner speeches should be short – never bore people with a _____ .

3. Many businessmen are driven by a _____ to succeed.

4. A _____ like Mr Cashman has no time for emotions.

5. _____ look elegant, but they are not comfortable to walk in.

6. A _____ was shouting at some passers-by.

7. The American civil rights movement had to fight against many _____ .

8. 'Love in Funsville' is a _____ about a group of teenagers falling in love.

C – D 9. On hearing Sue's joke Rex gave a _____ that made everyone turn around.

10. People with a _____ like a Ferrari should take extra care to drive responsibly.

11. Bruce Willis plays an ex-cop in a _____ with lots of car chases.

12. I think Janet's plan is excellent and I'll give it my _____ .

13. Being a _____ is not enough, if you can't put your good intentions into practice.

14. In summer I always dress casually in Bermuda shorts and a _____ .

15. Ron has an extremely _____ of the situation, he just blames everybody else.

16. You can't run a business on a day-to-day basis; what you need is a _____ .

Test 10

COMPOUND ADJECTIVES

_____

tight-fisted

_____

HIGH-MINDED and FAR-SIGHTED

Setzen Sie die zu den Definitionen passenden Adjektive zusammen.

| A | broad | fresh | hot | slow | **tight** |
| B | hard | short | starry | tight | two |

| A | blooded | faced | **fisted** | minded | witted |
| B | eyed | faced | hearted | lipped | tempered |

A 1. Someone who is mean and hates spending money is ▶ __**tight-fisted**__

   2. Emotional and easily excited ▶ _____

   3. A person who is young and healthy-looking is ▶ _____

   4. If you need plenty of time to understand something you are ▶ _____

   5. Willing to respect the opinions of others, tolerant and liberal ▶ _____

B 6. If you easily get angry for no good reason you are ▶ _____

   7. Someone who is indifferent to other people's suffering and feelings is ▶ _____

   8. If you cannot be believed or are insincere you are ▶ _____

   9. Hopeful and optimistic in an unrealistic and naive way ▶ _____

   10. Someone who refuses to give information or talk about something is ▶ _____

Test 11

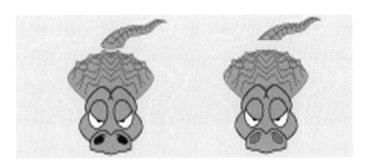

*Can you believe it? They're accusing me of the cold-blooded murder of a zebra! I'm a **reptile**, for heaven's sake – I AM cold-blooded.*

QUICK-WITTED SYNONYMS

Zusammengesetzte Adjektive haben oft übertragene Bedeutung: so ist ein **big-headed man** kein Mann mit einem großen Kopf, sondern ein **arroganter**, von sich eingenommener Zeitgenosse. Meist haben solche Zusammensetzungen auch einfache Adjektive als Synonyme (Worte gleicher oder ähnlicher Bedeutung). Führen Sie die Synonym-Paare zusammen.

A	aristocratic	conceited	**forgetful**	generous	rational	unfeeling
B	clumsy	cowardly	depressed	fair	idealistic	lively
C	confident	confused	embarrassed	gentle	insensitive	intelligent

A   absent-minded ____**forgetful**____

big-headed _____

big-hearted _____

blue-blooded _____

cold-blooded _____

cool-headed _____

B   even-handed _____

faint-hearted _____

flat-footed _____

high-spirited _____

high-principled _____

low-spirited _____

C   mild-mannered _____

muddle-headed _____

quick-witted _____

red-faced _____

sure-footed _____

thick-skinned _____

Test 12

COMPOUND ADJECTIVES

Nothing is fool-proof to . . . . . . a sufficiently talented fool.

GRAMMAR GURU
INSTANT WISDOM

BE GRAMMAR-CONSCIOUS

Die Adjektive in der grauen Zeile sind besonders produktiv in der Struktur: Substantiv + Adjektiv = Adjektiv. Verwenden Sie jedes der sechs Adjektive dreimal, um die Ausdrücke korrekt zu vervollständigen.

-conscious	-free	-proof	-related	-ridden	-rich
		✔			

bullet-	**proof**	vest	job-	_____	travel
child-	_____	lock	lead-	_____	petrol
cliché-	_____	political speech	meat-	_____	diet
debt-	_____	poor countries	oil-	_____	Gulf states
drug-	_____	crime	oxygen-	_____	air
guilt-	_____	neurotic	protein-	_____	nuts
health-	_____	fitness trainer	rain-	_____	anorak
image-	_____	movie star	safety-	_____	security officer
interest-	_____	loan	smoking-	_____	cancer

22

Test 13

A BREATHTAKING EXERCISE

Kombinieren Sie die Adjektive der grauen Box mit den Substantiven und vervollständigen Sie die Sätze.

| A | ear-splitting | English-speaking | figure-hugging | **labour-saving** | life-saving |
| B | breathtaking | epoch-making | head-turning | law-abiding | mouth-watering |

labour-saving device
_____ dress
_____ nations
_____ noise
_____ operation

_____ citizen
_____ desserts
_____ good looks
_____ event
_____ special effects

A 1. The washing machine is a **labour-saving device** that nobody would want to be without.

2. A _____ like a heart by-pass has become routine in the western world.

3. There is a special relationship between the _____ of America and Britain.

4. In her _____ actress Sashay caused a sensation at the film festival.

5. Doctors say that the _____ of a rock concert can damage your hearing.

B 6. The fall of the Berlin Wall was an _____ which fundamentally changed history.

7. Bond films are always full of _____ .

8. The food at 'The Ivy' is delicious, I particularly like their _____ .

9. No _____ has anything to fear from our new security measures.

10. Brad Pitt not only has _____ , he's also a talented actor.

Test 14

COMPOUND ADJECTIVES

_____   _____   _____

ACTION-PACKED and TAILOR-MADE

Substantiv + Past Participle (-ed/3. Form) = Adjektiv

Kombinieren Sie die zusammengesetzten Adjektive mit den
dazu passenden Substantiven und vervollständigen Sie die Sätze auf der gegenüberliegenden Seite.

action-packed	**film**	accidents	gift-wrapped	_____	beaches
alcohol-related	_____	avenue	home-made	_____	jacket
air-conditioned	_____	**film**	moth-eaten	_____	mountains
tailor-made	_____	hotel room	snow-covered	_____	present
tree-lined	_____	suit	sun-drenched	_____	soup
calcium-enriched	_____	flat	blood-stained	_____	cake
hand-written	_____	industries	computer-aided	_____	souvenirs
purpose-built	_____	letter	mass-produced	_____	shirt
star-studded	_____	milk	shark-infested	_____	design
state-owned	_____	show	sugar-coated	_____	waters

Sections: A, B, C, D

24

Test 15

VERVOLLSTÄNDIGEN SIE DIE SÄTZE MIT DEN AUSDRÜCKEN DER GEGENÜBERLIEGENDEN SEITE

A – B
1. 'The L.A. Squad' is an _____action-packed film_____ with lots of gun fights and punch-ups.

2. The ideal location for a house is in a quiet _____ not far from the centre.

3. The sun was unbearably hot so it felt good to return to my _____ .

4. _____ is supposed to make children's bones stronger.

5. Drinking and driving is dangerous, there are still too many _____ .

6. Old people should be able to live in a _____ that exactly suits their needs.

7. Beautifully sun-tanned and in an elegant _____ , Tom was a big hit with the ladies.

8. The privatisation of _____ in Britain has not always been a success.

9. After the flood of e-mails I get every day a _____ makes a welcome change.

10. 'Crazy' is a _____ which has been highly praised by theatre critics.

C – D
11. I've eaten in many good restaurants, but nothing beats my grandmother's _____ .

12. Look at Sid's _____ . Has he been fighting again?

13. An old tramp in a _____ shambled up to us and asked for a dollar.

14. Ken is trying to impress Julia - he's bought her roses and a huge _____ .

15. _____ is an important tool of the modern architect.

16. Al's promises are like a _____ – sweet from the outside but without any substance.

17. It's dangerous to swim in the _____ off the Australian coast.

18. All my friends brought me from Spain was one of those terrible _____ .

19. From the _____ of the Sierra Nevada to the _____ _____ of the Costa del Sol the Spanish province of Granada has something for everybody.

Test 16

COMPOUND ADJECTIVES

THE BIG-PRIZE TEST

Adjektiv (full) + Substantiv (length) = Adjektiv: full-length
Vervollständigen Sie die Sätze mit den zusammengesetzten Adjektiven.

big-prize 1. 'Who wants to be a millionaire?' was the ultimate ___**big-prize**___ game show of 2003.

early-warning 2. You should base a fire evacuation plan on a _____ scenario.

fair-weather 3. Our hospital needs an _____ unit for seriously ill patients.

first-class 4. I'm afraid Al is just a _____ friend who'll leave you in times of trouble.

intensive-care 5. We went to a _____ restaurant in Paris, the food was really delicious.

worst-case 6. Pain is the body's _____ system, it tells us that something is wrong.

five-star 7. I'm tired of soap operas, I'd like to see a proper _____ feature film.

full-length 8. Never put money into a _____ investment like shares in a gold mine!

high-fidelity 9. I hate _____ flights, after more than two hours in an aircraft I feel ill.

high-risk 10. We booked an exclusive _____ hotel for our next holiday.

hot-water 11. To really appreciate classical music you need a good _____ sound system.

long-haul 12. An old joke says: 'Europeans have sex, the English have _____ bottles.'

free-market 13. I had watched a _____ movie till two in the morning and was tired all day.

last-minute 14. Without a _____ solution to the AIDS problem, millions of people will die.

late-night 15. Watch out, you're driving in the wrong direction; this is a _____ street.

long-term 16. A _____ economy will always be superior to state planning.

multiple-choice 17. A _____ test gives you several answers, of which only one is correct.

one-way 18. My boss is driving me mad with his _____ changes to everything I do.

Test 17

 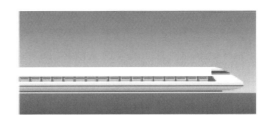 

A FIRST-CLASS HIGH-SPEED TEST

Bilden Sie zusammengesetzte Adjektive und kombinieren Sie diese mit den passenden Substantiven.

free	full	high	hot
long	**low**	real	single

air	distance	**fat**	life
parent	range	speed	time

balloon	eggs	experience	family
job	runner	train	**yoghurt**

1. I'm worried about Faye's new diet, all she eats is fruit, nuts and _____**low-fat yoghurt**_____.

2. I hate the idea of chickens suffering in small cages. I only buy _____.

3. The Eurostar is a _____ connecting Paris and London.

4. Travelling around the world in a _____ must be one of the last big adventures.

5. The London Marathon was won by Mito Mbele, a _____ from Kenya.

6. The film 'Escape' is based on the _____ of a pilot kidnapped by gangsters.

7. Marianne's is a typical _____ – she's divorced and lives with her two sons.

8. It feels good to have a proper _____ after years of unemployment.

Test 18

COMPOUND ADJECTIVES

_____ humour   _____ resuscitation   _____ attitude

UP-TO-DATE INFORMATION

Der Platz und die Funktion des Adjektivs kann auch von komplexen Wortzusammensetzungen eingenommen werden; das Englische macht von dieser Möglichkeit mit großem Erfindungsreichtum Gebrauch.

A	day-to-day	down-to-earth	happy-go-lucky
	mouth-to-mouth	round-the-clock	**up-to-date**
B	chicken-and-egg	fly-on-the-wall	head-in-the-sand
	rank-and-file	spur-of-the-moment	tongue-in-cheek

A 1. A top scientist always has _____**up-to-date**_____ information on what's happening in his field.

2. Our supermarket never closes, we offer a _____ service.

3. As a life guard at Palm Beach I have to be able to give _____ resuscitation.

4. Glen with his _____ attitude never plans anything in advance.

5. Zara is looking for a manager for the _____ running of her boutique in Soho.

6. I'm not interested in art and philosophy; I'm a practical _____ person.

B 7. I don't know what made me quit my job, it was a _____ decision.

8. Without the support of its _____ members no political party can survive.

9. With their _____ attitude US car makers ignored foreign competition for too long.

10. The English are famous for their subtle _____ humour.

11. In a new _____ documentary a camera team follows a paper boy on his daily round.

12. No job without experience, no experience without a job – a typical _____ situation.

28

A STATE-OF-THE-ART TEST!

Bilden Sie die korrekten Kombinationen und vervollständigen Sie mit diesen die Sätze.

A		B	
end-of-term	**technology**	fun-in-the-sun	chance
hit-and-run	school report	middle-of-the-road	holiday
nine-to-five	job	off-the-peg	cruise
on-the-spot	driver	once-in-a-lifetime	politics
state-of-the-art	**technology**	rags-to-riches	clothes
stop-and-go	traffic	round-the-world	career
	fine		

A 1. With the very best ___**state-of-the-art technology**___ the new X-8 is the world's best computer.

    2. The police are looking for the _____ who caused an accident last night.

    3. In the _____ of the rush hour it took us ages to get home.

    4. Ray was never ambitious, he's happy with his boring _____ in a bank.

    5. Al was caught speeding and had to pay an _____ to the police officers.

    6. A pupil's _____ reflects the results of all written tests.

B 7. With our lottery win we went on a _____ on a luxury ship.

    8. Our party stands for sensible _____ and avoids extremes.

    9. I love beaches and I love discos, so I booked a _____ in Spain.

    10. In a typical _____ Ian worked his way up from salesman to millionaire.

    11. You'll never get such an opportunity again, it's a _____ .

    12. I can't afford tailor-made dresses, I only wear _____ .

Test 20

COLLOCATION

_____ temperatures   _____ island   _____ snake

COOL COLLOCATIONS

Vervollständigen Sie die Sätze mit den korrekten „Partnern" der Substantive.

female	1. Thank you for your visit, now drive carefully and have a __**safe**__ journey.
freezing	2. The injection of drugs used to be a _____ factor in the spread of AIDS.
major	3. It was a _____ climb up the cliffs and my uncle was puffing heavily.
regular	4. _____ rain forests are home to an amazing variety of animals.
safe	5. I can't imagine how people can live in the _____ temperatures of Alaska.
solid	6. Jane Austen is the most well-known _____ novelist in English literature.
steep	7. After a year of temporary jobs I want to go back to a _____ income again.
tropical	8. Without the _____ support of his party a Prime Minister is powerless.
extensive	9. I have a _____ memory of the accident, but I can't remember the details.
hefty	10. Shakespeare with his _____ vocabulary introduced many new words.
peaceful	11. The cobra is one of the world's most dangerous _____ snakes.
poisonous	12. On the last night of the art festival they had a _____ fireworks display.
spectacular	13. The police reported a _____ demonstration with no incidents.
true	14. Marlon was caught speeding on the M1 and had to pay a _____ fine.
vague	15. Alister's new thriller is based on a _____ story from World War II.
wrong	16. I don't want to make a _____ decision which I'll regret later.

ADJECTIVE & NOUN PARTNERSHIPS

Führen Sie die Adjektiv-Substantiv-Kollokationen zusammen.

curly	**hair**	apology	brutal		breakdown
general		economy	intensive		care
global		election	keen		conclusion
high		**hair**	logical		intellect
humble		season	nervous		murder

gradual		beach	cancerous		pattern
illegal		development	fair		supporter
industrial		reaction	geometric		standard
instinctive		drugs	loyal		play
sandy		revolution	moral		tumour

gentle		baby	boundless		foundation
professional		breeze	first-class		perfume
new-born		footballer	foreseeable		ticket
hearty		state	fragrant		energy
totalitarian		welcome	solid		future

COLLOCATION

Test 22

 _____ sea    _____ damage    _____ rain

CHOOSE THE CORRECT ADJECTIVE

Nur eines der jeweiligen Adjektive ist der korrekte „Partner" für das Substantiv im Satz.

1. These shoes are too _____**tight**_____ . ○ slim ○ constrained ✓ **tight**

2. Pam said there was a fire, but it was a _____ alarm. ○ false ○ wrong ○ incorrect

3. The _____ decision rests with Mr Bigboss. ○ terminal ○ conclusive ○ final

4. It is my _____ belief that Sue is right. ○ fast ○ solid ○ firm

5. This watch is made of _____ gold. ○ massive ○ pure ○ solid

6. The _____ sea caused the ship to sink. ○ raw ○ rough ○ strong

7. I learnt to ski on a _____ slope in the Alps. ○ gentle ○ light ○ soft

8. What you say is a _____ exaggeration. ○ coarse ○ rough ○ gross

9. The _____ truth is that Sam lied to you. ○ harsh ○ tough ○ hard

10. Mark is in bed with a _____ cold. ○ strong ○ heavy ○ hefty

11. This cooking oil is of _____ quality. ○ weak ○ deep ○ poor

12. The planet Mars is visible to the _____ eye. ○ mere ○ naked ○ normal

13. In Spain it is _____ practice to stay up late. ○ usual ○ ordinary ○ common

14. The accident caused _____ damage to my car. ○ serious ○ heavy ○ hard

Test 23

CHOOSE THE CORRECT ADJECTIVE

Nur eines der jeweiligen Adjektive ist der korrekte „Partner" für das Substantiv im Satz.

1. Blub should go on a diet, he's much too _____ . ○ thick ○ fat ○ gross

2. Thank you for your _____ reply to our letter. ○ rapid ○ fast ○ prompt

3. Without _____ guitars there'd be no rock music. ○ electric ○ electrical ○ electronic

4. Ray is a _____ man. ○ beautiful ○ pretty ○ handsome

5. We had a very _____ conversation about art. ○ lively ○ alive ○ living

6. I love my aunt's _____ potato soup. ○ tasteful ○ tasty ○ tasting

7. Never dive into the _____ end of the pool. ○ even ○ flat ○ shallow

8. We offer a _____ choice of flavours. ○ wide ○ broad ○ big

9. That was a very _____ discussion. ○ fertile ○ fruitful ○ fruity

10. Barry needed _____ treatment. ○ medicinal ○ medic ○ medical

11. To my _____ relief Kim survived her illness. ○ large ○ big ○ immense

12. It is a _____ honour to meet you. ○ great ○ big ○ large

13. There's a _____ connection between drugs and crime. ○ close ○ narrow ○ near

14. Paul died in a _____ accident on the M1. ○ deadly ○ fatal ○ deathly

15. There is a _____ chance that we might succeed. ○ remote ○ far ○ distant

16. Drinking causes _____ damage to the brain. ○ ever-lasting ○ steady ○ permanent

17. Driving is fun on the _____ roads of America. ○ broad ○ wide ○ big

18. The officer took a _____ look at my passport. ○ speedy ○ fast ○ quick

19. We cycled down a _____ lane. ○ narrow ○ tight ○ close

20. _____ rain caused flooding on the roads. ○ dense ○ strong ○ heavy

Test 24

COLLOCATION

COLLOCATION TRIOS · 1

Finden Sie die Adjektiv-Partner, die jeweils zu allen drei Substantiven passen.

A	great	**high**	hot	intensive	local	massive
B	accurate	low	narrow	powerful	serious	sharp

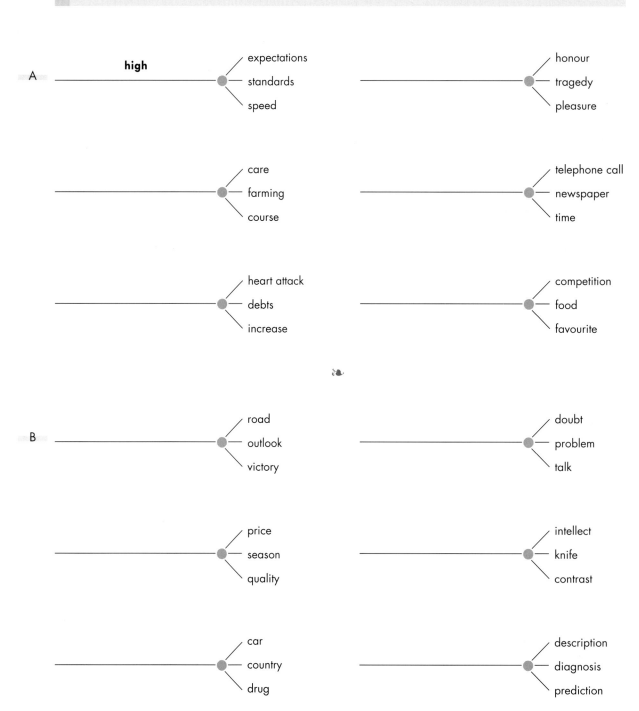

COLLOCATION TRIOS • 2

Nun zur schwierigeren Variante: Keine Aufteilung in A und B.

| ancient | bitter | broad | clear | close | deep |
| diplomatic | fresh | hearty | personal | private | wide |

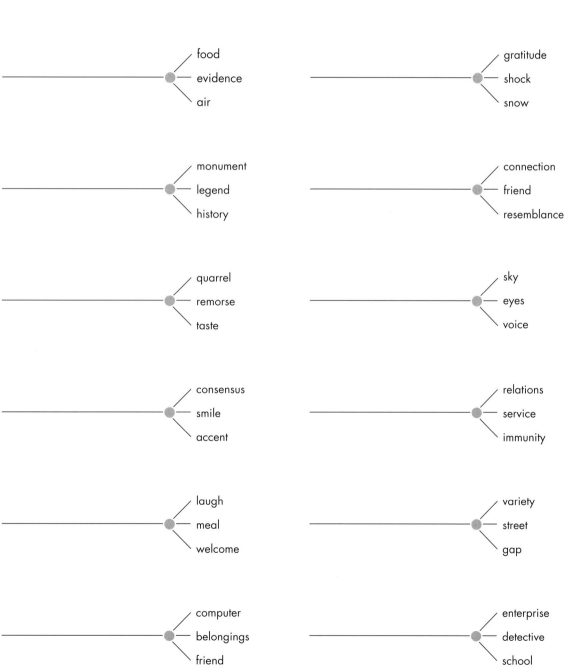

Test 26

COLLOCATION

Tell me, Mr Gandhi –
What do you think of Western civilization?

I think
it would be a good idea.

FIND THE HAPPY MEDIUM

Bestimmte Adjektiv+Substantiv-Kombinationen haben sich zu eigenen neuen Ausdrücken – FIXED PAIRS – verfestigt. Kombinieren Sie die folgenden Adjektive und Substantive zu neuen Wörtern und vervollständigen Sie die Sätze.

A	**happy**	identical	previous	primary	professional
B	final	moral	racial	royal	social

A	advice	marriage	**medium**	school	twins
B	decision	mobility	palace	prejudice	support

A 1. Alcohol is good for you, but don't drink too much – a glass of red wine a day is a ____**happy medium**____.

2. Bob's new wife has two children from a _____.

3. Amy and Joan are _____; it's very hard to tell them apart.

4. You should take _____ before selling your house. Why not ask a lawyer?

5. In some countries children start _____ when they are five.

B 6. Windsor Castle is the largest inhabited _____ in the world.

7. Tim has lost his job; I'll go and see if I can give him some _____.

8. The politics of Apartheid were built on _____ against South Africa's black people.

9. I'd like to have a company car, but of course the _____ lies with my boss.

10. In America there are no class barriers and _____ is the norm.

ADJECTIVE & NOUN · FIXED PAIRS

Viele deutsche Nominalzusammensetzungen werden im Englischen durch Kombinationen aus Adjektiv+Substantiv wiedergegeben wie z.B. *Endphase* → *final stage*.
Bilden Sie die englischen Entsprechungen der deutschen Zusammensetzungen.

basic	Endphase ▸	**final stage**	clothing
constitutional	Flutwelle ▸	_____	court
domestic	Grundlohn ▸	_____	delinquency
final	Haushaltshilfe ▸	_____	help
juvenile	Jugendkriminalität ▸	_____	magazine
monthly	Monatsmagazin ▸	_____	**stage**
occupational	Schutzkleidung ▸	_____	therapy
protective	Verfassungsgericht ▸	_____	wages
tidal	Verhaltenstherapie ▸	_____	wave
annual	Außenpolitik ▸	_____	disease
foreign	Gentechnik ▸	_____	election
genetical	Geschlechtskrankheit ▸	_____	energy
judicial	Jahresurlaub ▸	_____	engineering
musical	Justizirrtum ▸	_____	error
parliamentary	Musikinstrument ▸	_____	holiday
preferential	Parlamentswahl ▸	_____	instrument
solar	Sonnenenergie ▸	_____	policy
venereal	Vorzugsbehandlung ▸	_____	treatment

Test 27

Test 28

COLLOCATION

a _____ doctor   _____ rain   a _____ pair

WITH FLYING COLOURS

Komplettieren Sie die FIXED PAIRS mit den Partizipien aus der grauen Box.

crowning	1. Vanessa passed her exam with __**flying**__ colours and without the slightest hitch.
driving	2. Tom thought he was in love with Susan, but it was just a _____ fancy.
finishing	3. Life for women under the Taliban regime in Afghanistan was a _____ hell.
flying	4. Winning the Nobel prize is the _____ glory for any writer.
living	5. I've almost finished my essay, I've just got to put the _____ touches to it.
passing	6. Everybody knows Tim is crazy about Emily, it's a _____ joke.
rolling	7. Papa was a _____ stone, wherever he laid his head was his home. (song lyric)
standing	8. A woman is often the actual _____ force behind a successful man.
blazing	9. Beryl bought a _____ pair of Chinese vases for her living room.
gaping	10. Our car broke down and we had to walk through the _____ rain.
matching	11. Watching Hitler's speeches on film, you see that he was a _____ lunatic.
pouring	12. Mother Teresa was a _____ example of what you can do to help others.
practising	13. Marion and Paul split up after they had a _____ row over money.
raving	14. The bullfighter was carried out of the arena with a _____ wound in his leg.
rising	15. As a _____ doctor I just don't have enough time for medical research.
shining	16. After his first exhibition Paul is the new _____ star of the art world.

Test 29

LIVING PROOF

Führen Sie die FIXED PAIRS zusammen und komplettieren Sie die Sätze.

burning _____ ambition

living _____**proof**_____ guest

opposing _____ invitation

paying _____ **proof**

roaring _____ success

standing _____ views

deafening _____ countries

developing _____ creatures

flying _____ noise

living _____ similarity

striking _____ start

winning _____ team

A 1. Bill Gates is _____**living proof**_____ of the fact that you can become a billionaire by your own effort.

2. As a highly motivated tennis player Wayne has a _____ to win Wimbledon.

3. The new musical is a _____ . All shows have been sold out for weeks.

4. I don't like hotels, I prefer to stay in private homes as a _____ .

5. Come and visit us whenever you like, you know you have a _____ .

6. Stella and John have _____ on immigration, she's for it and he's against it.

B 7. _____ can only prosper, if we open our markets to their products.

8. We should respect not just our fellow men but all other _____ as well.

9. 'Never change a _____ ', is an old saying from the world of sports.

10. Ken has got off to a _____ in his new job, he's already been given his first promotion.

11. Don't you think Sue bears a _____ to her sister? – No wonder, they're twins.

12. Colin covered his ears against the _____ of a low-flying plane.

39

Test 30

COLLOCATION

_____ policeman   _____ instruments   _____ craftsman

MIXED BAG

Komplettieren Sie die FIXED PAIRS mit den Adjektiven aus der grauen Box.

fixed	1. The guests were a _____**mixed**_____ bag, from penniless artists to affluent bankers.
hushed	2. _____ crime is one of the biggest problems in Russia.
licensed	3. Joel was arrested in a case of _____ identity, but they soon released him.
mistaken	4. Hotels with a _____ bar have a special permission to sell alcoholic drinks.
mixed	5. I can't afford to buy a flat in London, so I live in _____ accommodation.
organised	6. In police reports a homeless person is described as 'of no _____ abode'.
rented	7. Joan spoke in a _____ voice so as not to wake the children.
૨૪	૨૪
gifted	8. The violin is the most popular _____ instrument after the guitar.
limited	9. 'Bobby' is a popular nickname for an English _____ policeman.
mixed	10. No amateur should lay a parquet floor, always employ a _____ craftsman.
skilled	11. I don't need a luxury limousine, I'm quite happy with a cheap _____ car.
stringed	12. A copy of a special _____ edition of Shaw's 'Pygmalion' was sold for £500.
uniformed	13. I have _____ feelings about emigrating to Canada. I think I'll miss England.
used	14. They tested Emma's IQ and found that she is an exceptionally _____ child.

Test 31

MAKE A CONCENTRATED EFFORT

Führen Sie die FIXED PAIRS zusammen und komplettieren Sie die Definitionen.

A	broken	**concentrated**	furnished	pointed	registered	scheduled
B	armed	charmed	extended	hired	mixed	packed

A	apartment	**effort**	flight	home	letter	remark
B	blessing	family	forces	hand	life	lunch

A 1. A determined and sincere attempt to achieve something ▸ __**concentrated effort**__

   2. Something you say in a way that shows your criticism ▸ _____

   3. An unhappy family with separated or divorced parents ▸ _____

   4. A special form of postal service to insure the item sent ▸ _____

   5. A place to rent with all the furniture already in place ▸ _____

   6. A plane service flying regularly at the same time ▸ _____

B 7. Food carried in a bag or container to school or work ▸ _____

   8. The military forces (army, navy, air force) of a country ▸ _____

   9. Something that has advantages as well as disadvantages ▸ _____

  10. Someone who is employed to help on a farm ▸ _____

  11. If you are always lucky even in difficult situations you have a ▸ _____

  12. Not just parents and children, but all other relatives ▸ _____

Test 32

SYNONYMS

miserable – _____   tasty – _____   precious – _____

ADJECTIVE SYNONYMS

Synonyme sind Worte gleicher oder ähnlicher Bedeutung. Führen Sie die Synonympaare zusammen.

accurate	**precise**	awkward	lazy	delicious
bizarre		comfortable	modest	powerful
clumsy		original	precious	humble
cosy		**precise**	simple	idle
creative		remote	strong	elementary
distant		weird	tasty	valuable
genuine		fortunate	curious	considerate
ghastly		nude	exhausted	ideal
loud		unhappy	honest	nosy
lucky		real	perfect	obstinate
miserable		noisy	stubborn	tired
naked		grim	tactful	truthful

42

Test 33

COOL, CALM and COLLECTED

Finden Sie jeweils zwei Synonyme aus der grauen Box für die folgenden Adjektive.

A
- ○ appropriate ○ boring ○ brainy ○ **calm** ○ **collected** ○ competent
- ○ eager ○ efficient ○ intelligent ○ keen ○ right ○ tedious

B
- ○ affluent ○ fashionable ○ fierce ○ helpful ○ orderly ○ renowned
- ○ savage ○ sociable ○ stylish ○ tidy ○ wealthy ○ well-known

A

able _____ _____

clever _____ _____

cool **calm** **collected**

correct _____ _____

dull _____ _____

enthusiastic _____ _____

B

elegant _____ _____

famous _____ _____

friendly _____ _____

neat _____ _____

rich _____ _____

wild _____ _____

SYNONYMS

Test 34

○ handsome   ○ pretty   ✓ rich   ○ beautiful

ODD ONE OUT

Jeweils eines der Adjektive in jeder Reihe ist KEIN Synonym.

1.	○ cosy	○ comfortable	○ harsh	○ snug
2.	○ faint	○ feeble	○ weak	○ unhappy
3.	○ brutal	○ sadistic	○ nasty	○ proper
4.	○ kind	○ good-natured	○ tired	○ thoughtful
5.	○ lucky	○ happy	○ glad	○ cheerful
6.	○ cheap	○ idle	○ lazy	○ sluggish
7.	○ silly	○ foolish	○ stupid	○ serious
8.	○ careless	○ lively	○ quick	○ alert
9.	○ precise	○ tasteful	○ exact	○ correct
10.	○ pure	○ expensive	○ clean	○ spotless
11.	○ delicious	○ false	○ incorrect	○ wrong
12.	○ sad	○ unhappy	○ content	○ miserable
13.	○ fit	○ helpful	○ healthy	○ sound
14.	○ dull	○ strong	○ boring	○ tiresome
15.	○ curious	○ prying	○ nosy	○ generous
16.	○ modest	○ crazy	○ humble	○ shy
17.	○ massive	○ dangerous	○ huge	○ enormous
18.	○ unusual	○ dirty	○ rare	○ infrequent

Test 35

A PLEASANT / AGREEABLE TEST

Führen Sie die Synonympaare zusammen und tragen sie diese in die Sätze ein.

A	adult	continuous	permanent	plain	**pleasant**	rigid	well-behaved
B	arrogant	basic	busy	ideal	remote	sacred	stable

A	**agreeable**	ceaseless	grown-up	inflexible	lasting	obvious	polite
B	active	conceited	distant	fundamental	holy	perfect	solid

A 1. We spent a very ___**pleasant**___ / ___**agreeable**___ afternoon in London's wonderful Hyde Park.

2. My niece is a very _____ / _____ young lady and we all like her.

3. We need a _____ / _____ solution to this problem.

4. Europe's labour laws are much more _____ / _____ than those of America.

5. It was quite _____ / _____ to the police that Jake was lying.

6. Stop acting like a child and behave like an _____ / a _____ person.

7. The _____ / _____ roar of a nearby motorway drove me crazy.

B 8. At some _____ / _____ time in the future the sun will burn itself out.

9. Freedom of speech is one of the _____ / _____ rights in a democracy.

10. Martha is the _____ / _____ wife for Mark – they have so much in common.

11. Honesty is a _____ / _____ foundation for all human relationships.

12. Marco's _____ / _____ belief that he's always right is quite ridiculous.

13. Mary is seventy, but still runs her own company and leads a very _____ / _____ life.

14. On our Indian tour we went to see the _____ / _____ shrine of the tiger god.

ANTONYMS

Test 36

DEAD or ALIVE

Antonyme sind Worte von entgegengesetzter Bedeutung. Führen Sie die Gegensatzpaare zusammen.

alive	**dead**	slow		guilty		different
early		dead		hard		long
empty		late		heavy		soft
fast		high		mean		light
low		full		short		innocent
rare		common		similar		generous

bright		abstract		idle		married
calm		dark		nice		busy
cheap		dirty		simple		foolish
clean		nervous		single		nasty
concrete		expensive		wasteful		complicated
harmless		dangerous		wise		economical

Test 37

The trouble with telling an amusing story is . . .

. . . that it reminds someone else of a boring one.
Groucho Marx

MORE ANTONYMS

Führen Sie die Gegensatzpaare zusammen.

A
- ○ alcoholic ○ ancient ○ electric
- ○ sharp ○ stale ○ **tame**

⇔

A
- ○ acoustic ○ blunt ○ fresh
- ○ modern ○ soft ○ **wild**

B
- ○ amusing ○ easy ○ natural
- ○ permanent ○ tall ○ wide

B
- ○ artificial ○ boring ○ difficult
- ○ narrow ○ short ○ temporary

A
- a **tame** animal ⇔ a **wild** animal
- _____ bread ⇔ _____ bread
- an _____ drink ⇔ a _____ drink
- an _____ guitar ⇔ an _____ guitar
- _____ history ⇔ _____ history
- a _____ knife ⇔ a _____ knife

B
- _____ light ⇔ _____ light
- a _____ road ⇔ a _____ road
- a _____ solution ⇔ a _____ solution
- an _____ story ⇔ a _____ story
- an _____ task ⇔ a _____ task
- a _____ man ⇔ a _____ man

ANTONYMS

Test 38

FIND THE ANTONYM PAIRS

Jeweils zwei der Adjektive in jeder Reihe sind Antonyme.

1.	○ **full**	○ modern	○ **empty**	○ cheap
2.	○ rough	○ weak	○ creative	○ smooth
3.	○ honest	○ bored	○ strong	○ weak
4.	○ loud	○ shallow	○ deep	○ ugly
5.	○ dark	○ hungry	○ full	○ pleasant
6.	○ arrogant	○ humble	○ tired	○ intelligent
7.	○ tall	○ thirsty	○ polite	○ rude
8.	○ quiet	○ dark	○ pretty	○ noisy
9.	○ tiny	○ mild	○ huge	○ strange
10.	○ clumsy	○ skilful	○ curious	○ dry
11.	○ vast	○ serious	○ funny	○ reluctant
12.	○ serious	○ sweet	○ slow	○ sour
13.	○ soft	○ absent	○ rich	○ present
14.	○ hot	○ generous	○ strange	○ familiar
15.	○ common	○ rare	○ young	○ sad
16.	○ competent	○ kind	○ malicious	○ bankrupt
17.	○ wealthy	○ afraid	○ poor	○ slim
18.	○ expensive	○ grand	○ loose	○ tight

FIND TWO ANTONYMS

Finden Sie jeweils zwei Antonyme aus der grauen Box für die folgenden Adjektive.

A
- damp
- depressed
- **frantic**
- honest
- obscure
- sad
- safe
- secure
- trustworthy
- vague
- wet
- **wild**

B
- difficult
- eager
- essential
- flawless
- hard
- healthy
- keen
- loud
- noisy
- perfect
- relevant
- well

A

calm ⟺ **frantic** — **wild**

cheerful ⟺ _____ — _____

clear ⟺ _____ — _____

dangerous ⟺ _____ — _____

deceitful ⟺ _____ — _____

dry ⟺ _____ — _____

B

easy ⟺ _____ — _____

faulty ⟺ _____ — _____

quiet ⟺ _____ — _____

reluctant ⟺ _____ — _____

sick ⟺ _____ — _____

unimportant ⟺ _____ — _____

Test 40

ADJECTIVES AS NOUNS

A TEST FOR THE INTELLIGENT

Bestimmte substantivierte Adjektive bezeichnen eine Gruppe von Menschen, die eine gemeinsame Eigenschaft besitzen: *the intelligent = (all) intelligent people*; sie stehen mit dem bestimmten Artikel und ohne Plural –s.
Vervollständigen Sie die Sätze mit den substantivierten Adjektiven aus der grauen Box.

A	beautiful	blind	famous	homeless	injured	poor	rich
B	dead	elderly	hungry	living	sick	unemployed	young

A
1. The luxury hotels of the Swiss Alps are a playgound of _____ and __**the famous**__.
2. Some traffic lights have a sound signal, so that _____ know when to cross the street.
3. Ambulance crews are trained to give first aid to _____.
4. When the rich make war it's _____ that die. (Jean-Paul Sartre)
5. In winter the city of Stockholm makes old railway carriages available to _____.
6. The innocent and _____ have no enemy but time. (W. B. Yeats)

B
7. It will take a massive economic upswing to create jobs for _____.
8. When he could no longer look after himself Grandpa moved into a home for _____.
9. Can't you be quiet, for once? You're making enough noise to wake up _____.
10. Sue had a really nasty accident; she's lucky she's still among _____.
11. I love teaching, working with _____ is never boring.
12. Mother Teresa's aim was to feed _____ and build hospitals for _____.

Test 41

The worst thing about getting old . . . . . . is that it takes so long.
Bob Hope

MAY THE BEST PERSON WIN

Anders als im Deutschen können substantivierte Adjektive im Englischen nur Allgemeinbegriffe oder Gruppen in ihrer Gesamtheit bezeichnen; für Einzelpersonen, Teilgruppen oder Teilaspekte gelten folgende Muster:

Derek ist ein **Netter**. → Derek is a **nice boy / man / person / individual**.

Das **Gute** an Mike ist sein Humor. → The **good thing** about Mike is his sense of humour.

Übersetzen Sie nach obigem Muster.

1. Das Wichtigste ist, dass wir glücklich sind. _____

2. Geld ist das Einzige, was ich brauche. _____

3. Übergewichtige haben oft Diabetes. _____

4. Das Schönste im Leben ist die Liebe. _____

5. Das Gute an Susan ist ihre Verlässlichkeit. _____

6. Das Ganze ist eine Lüge. _____

7. Ein Reicher hat keine Probleme. _____

8. Ein Kranker oder Behinderter braucht Hilfe. _____

9. Möge der Beste gewinnen. _____

10. Ein Toter verdient Respekt. _____

11. Wir dürfen keinen Unschuldigen verurteilen. _____

12. Mary half einem Blinden über die Straße. _____

ADVERBS

← *Helen plays beautifully.*

Helen is beautiful. →

ADVERBS

ADJEKTIV:	Helen ist schön.	Helen is beautiful.
ADVERB:	Helen spielt schön.	Helen plays beautifully.

ADJEKTIVE (Eigenschaftswörter) beschreiben, wie jemand oder etwas ist, sie bestimmen ein Substantiv (eine Person oder eine Sache) oder ein Pronomen.

Helen is beautiful. – Tom is a careful driver. – They were happy. – She is polite.

ADVERBIEN hingegen dienen der näheren Bestimmung von:

a. Verben, d.h. der näheren Umstände der Handlung

Helen plays beautifully. – Tom drives carefully.   ▶ TEST 42

Bestimmte Verben treten dabei in typischen „Partnerschaften" mit bestimmten Adverbien auf (man nennt dieses gemeinsame Auftreten „Kollokation")

welcome warmly – applaud enthusiastically – attack violently   ▶ TEST 43

b. Adjektiven

This book is terribly dull. – Samantha is enormously successful.   ▶ TEST 44

Bestimmte Adjektive treten dabei in typischen „Partnerschaften" mit bestimmten Adverbien auf (man nennt dieses gemeinsame Auftreten „Kollokation")

absolutely right – clearly visible – exactly alike   ▶ TESTS 45 – 47

c. anderen Adverbien

Helen plays extremely beautifully. – Mike behaved perfectly sensibly.

d. ganzen Sätzen („Satzadverbien")

Happily, there hasn't been a burglary in our village for years.
Finally, I would like to thank you for your attention.   ▶ TEST 50

ADVERBIEN AUF '– LY'

Die Mehrzahl der englischen Adverbien werden durch Anhängen von -ly aus Adjektiven abgeleitet; dabei ist zu beachten:

1. **Da im Deutschen Adjektive und Adverbien die gleiche Form haben, ist das Vergessen des -ly ein häufiger Fehler; um diesen zu vermeiden, muss man fragen: Bezieht man sich (mit Adjektiv) auf ein Substantiv oder (mit Adverb) auf ein Verb oder Adjektiv?** ▶ TEST 48

2. **Andererseits behalten nicht wenige Adverbien die Adjektivform (ohne '-ly') bei**
   Take it easy. – We worked hard. – Selina drives very fast. ▶ TEST 53

3. **Vorsicht bei bestimmten Verben (Linking Verbs), die auf Zustände oder Eigenschaften des Subjekts oder Objekts verweisen. Diese werden mit einem Adjektiv verbunden.**
   You look great. – This pie smells nice and tastes delicious. – I feel tired. ▶ TESTS 54 & 55

BILDUNG DER ADVERBIEN MIT -LY

slow → slowly	loud → loudly	beautiful → beautifully
exact → exactly	sharp → sharply	independent → independently

Weiter ist zu beachten:

Adjektive auf '-y' bilden Adverbien auf '-ily'

happy → happily	dry → drily	noisy → noisily	lucky → luckily
greedy → greedily	goofy → goofily	rowdy → rowdily	witty → wittily

Ausnahmen: coy → coyly; shy → shyly; wry → wryly

die Endungen -ble, -ple, -tle werden zu: -bly, -ply, -tly

gentle → gently	terrible → terribly	unmistakable → unmistakably
ample → amply	humble → humbly	unforgettable → unforgettably

Adjektive auf '-ic' bilden Adverbien auf '-ically'

tragic → tragically   basic → basically   characteristic → characteristically

Ausnahme: public → publicly

bei Adjektiven auf '-ly' werden Umschreibungen verwendet

friendly → in a friendly way   silly → in a silly manner

Das Adverb von 'good' ist 'well'

good → well   – Helen plays the flute very well.

Bei 'true', 'due' und whole' entfällt das stumme -e:

true → truly   due → duly   whole → wholly

Adverbien werden stets mit MORE und MOST gesteigert

slowly → more slowly → most slowly; successfully → more successfully → most successfully

Test 42

ADVERBS

I'm not prejudiced – I hate everybody equally.

W.C. Fields

ANALYSE THIS TEST CLOSELY!

Vervollständigen Sie die Sätze mit den Adverbien aus der grauen Box.

accidentally	1. The audience was delighted and applauded ___**wildly**___ at the end of the play.
closely	2. Good investors analyse the market _____ before they buy any shares.
easily	3. Sheila opened the door and greeted me _____ with a hug.
gently	4. No, that's not correct. I'm afraid I _____ disagree with you there.
seriously	5. Tobacco _____ damages your health. (EU health warning)
totally	6. Paul _____ tripped over a stone and fell.
warmly	7. Annie has a lot of money and can _____ afford a new car.
wildly	8. It was an extremely valuable vase; I took it _____ out of the box.
confidently	9. Mrs Summer arranged the flowers _____ and with great care.
constantly	10. It was _____ raining on our holiday, we didn't have a single sunny day.
correctly	11. The police _____ accused Jim of theft, but his alibi proved his innocence.
falsely	12. Our team is in great shape and we _____ expect to win this match.
fully	13. The whole thing is a misunderstanding. I can _____ explain everything.
prettily	14. I would _____ recommend you to read John Updike's new novel.
quickly	15. Roy realised that he wasn't welcome and _____ withdrew.
strongly	16. Sitting _____ greatly reduces tiredness and back pain.

54

Test 43

VERB & ADVERB PARTNERSHIPS

Bestimmte Adverbien treten typischerweise zusammen mit bestimmten Verben auf (Kollokation).
Stellen Sie die korrekten Kombinationen her und vervollständigen Sie damit die Sätze.

| A | clash | laugh | listen | **remember** | travel |
| B | arrive | dance | give | speak | watch |

| A | attentively | happily | separately | violently | **vividly** |
| B | curiously | generously | gracefully | safely | softly |

A   1. I _____**remember vividly**_____ how Terry had a row with the waiter at our holiday hotel.

2. The students were fascinated by the lecture and _____.

3. Fifty people were injured when demonstrators _____ with the police.

4. The children _____ when the clown gave them a present each.

5. The President and the Vice-President always _____ in case of an accident.

B   6. We are collecting money for the local kindergarten, please _____.

7. The audience _____ as the magician put a rabbit in a box.

8. It was a long journey, but at last we _____ at my sister's house.

9. '_____ and carry a big stick,' was President Roosevelt's motto.

10. The ballerina _____ to the music of 'Swan Lake'.

55

ADVERBS

Test 44

FOR HIGHLY INTELLIGENT PEOPLE ONLY

Adverbien zur Bestimmung von Adjektiven: Vervollständigen Sie die Sätze mit den Adverbien aus der grauen Box.

A

- boringly
- cleverly
- excitingly
- locally
- immensely
- pleasantly

1. As an _____ successful businessman Bill Gates has many enemies.
2. 'Mind' is a stimulating magazine famous for its _____ written articles.
3. I always do the same thing at my job, everything is so _____ familiar.
4. To guarantee freshness we only serve _____ caught fish at our restaurant.
5. I'll never forget my first trip to New York, everything was so _____ new.
6. I was _____ surprised when a young man offered his seat to me on the bus.

B

- absolutely
- densely
- **highly**
- perfectly
- privately
- utterly

7. Kate's daughter is **highly** intelligent and has been admitted to Oxford.
8. We had a lovely ferry crossing, the sea was _____ calm.
9. I'm sure that is his address; I'm _____ convinced of it.
10. It was _____ irresponsible of Dan to let his son drive his car without a licence.
11. Hong Kong is one of the most _____ populated places on our planet.
12. Mustique is a _____ owned island, which you can hire for $150,000 a week.

C

- brutally
- extremely
- heavily
- politically
- spotlessly
- totally

13. It is not considered _____ correct to make jokes about minority groups.
14. The new film is _____ popular. It has already broken all box office records.
15. James became almost _____ blind when his eye operation went wrong.
16. Donna is very houseproud, her kitchen is always _____ clean.
17. The only way to tell John the truth was to be _____ honest.
18. I am _____ indebted to you for helping us so much.

Nothing is fool-proof to . . . *. . . a sufficiently talented fool.*

CLEARLY VISIBLE WORD PARTNERSHIPS

Bestimmte Adverbien treten typischerweise zusammen mit bestimmten Adjektiven auf (Kollokation). Stellen Sie die korrekten Kombinationen her und vervollständigen Sie damit die Sätze.

A	acutely	**clearly**	dazzlingly	hideously	vitally
B	carefully	genuinely	grossly	richly	scrupulously

A	aware	bright	important	ugly	**visible**
B	decorated	honest	interested	overweight	planned

A 1. Mars is ___**clearly visible**___ to the naked eye on a clear night.

2. Ben suddenly became _____ of the fact that he had made a terrible mistake.

3. What a _____ building! It makes you sick just to look at it, a real eyesore.

4. Getting that government contract is _____ for the survival of the company.

5. The driver was blinded by the _____ sunshine as he came out of the tunnel.

B 6. Only _____ customers will be able to test-drive the new Rolls Royce model.

7. I never saw so many fat people as in Florida, even the kids were _____ .

8. To succeed in an election a party must have a _____ strategy.

9. My father was _____ . I don't think he told a single lie in his entire life.

10. I love Bavaria's baroque churches with their _____ interiors.

ADVERBS

Test 46

ABSOLUTELY CORRECT

Bilden Sie die korrekten Kombinationen aus Adverb + Adjektiv und vervollständigen Sie die Sätze.

elegantly	dressed	beautiful
ideally	_____	committed
slightly	_____	damaged
strikingly	_____	dressed
wholeheartedly	_____	suited

deadly	_____	different
eternally	_____	grateful
fatally	_____	serious
radically	_____	possible
theoretically	_____	injured

A 1. In France it is quite important to be _____ **elegantly dressed** _____ if you want to succeed in life.

2. Mandela was _____ to ending apartheid in South Africa.

3. Ned has all the qualifications and the experience, he's _____ to the job.

4. The table was _____, but it was so cheap that we bought it.

5. Di looked so _____ in her new dress that we all gasped in amazement.

B 6. Modern Europe is _____ to the war-torn continent of the last century.

7. It is _____ but highly unlikely that man will ever live on Mars.

8. The accident victim was _____ and was dead on arrival at the hospital.

9. The US is always _____ when it threatens someone with military action.

10. I really can't thank you enough; I'll be _____ to you.

ADVERB & ADJECTIVE PARTNERSHIPS

Bilden Sie Kombinationen aus Adverb + Adjektiv, um die deutschen Ausdrücke zu übersetzen.

Adverb	Deutsch	Englisch	Adjektiv
badly	entfernt verwandt	**distantly related**	exaggerated
carefully	geistig behindert		furnished
distantly	glücklich verheiratet		handicapped
fully	hochintelligent		ill
grossly	maßlos übertrieben		intelligent
happily	schlecht bezahlt		married
highly	sorgfältig geplant		paid
mentally	unheilbar krank		planned
scientifically	voll möbliert (Wohnung)		proven
terminally	wissenschaftlich bewiesen		**related**
deeply	demokratisch gewählt		different
democratically	frisch gemahlen (Kaffee)		elected
environmentally	gut informiert		fit
freshly	hochqualifiziert		friendly
fully	körperlich gesund		ground
fundamentally	umweltfreundlich		informed
highly	voll funktionsfähig		operational
physically	weitgereist		qualified
well	zutiefst besorgt		travelled
widely	zutiefst verschieden		worried

ADVERBS

ADJECTIVE or ADVERB?

| ADJEKTIV: | Helen ist schön. | Helen is beautiful. |
| ADVERB: | Helen spielt schön. | Helen plays beautifully. |

ADJEKTIVE beschreiben Substantive (Personen oder Sachen): wie jemand oder etwas ist

Helen is beautiful. – Tom is a careful driver. – They were happy. – I feel fine.

ADVERBIEN dienen der näheren Bestimmung von

a. **Verben**   Helen plays beautifully. – Tom drives carefully.

b. **Adjektiven**   This book is terribly dull.

c. **Adverbien**   Helen plays extremely beautifully.

ADJECTIVE or ADVERB?

Verwenden Sie die richtigen Formen.

1. It's better to travel _____ (hopeful) than to arrive. (R. L. Stevenson)

2. Aida's movements were _____ (graceful) as she moved _____ (extreme, slow) around the room. She was a very _____ (attractive) woman.

3. Suddenly it started to rain and we _____ (quick) went inside.

4. It is _____ (moral) wrong to lie to people who trust you.

5. Max is _____ (good) at English, and his wife speaks English very _____ (good), too.

6. Maria has a _____ (beautiful) shaped face and _____ (shiny) hair.

7. They fell _____ (deep) in love, knew they were _____ (true) made for each other, married on a _____ (sunny) day in May and lived _____ (happy) ever after.

8. The room was _____ (bad) ventilated, I opened the door to get some _____ (fresh) air.

9. Buckingham Palace stands _____ (majestic) at the end of the Mall.

Test 48

10. This programme is new and has been developed _____ (specific) for teenagers.

11. Mick and Jerry are both _____ (extreme, successful) solicitors.

12. The weather was _____ (frightful) wet, I felt _____ (miserable) and cold.

13. The Minister spoke _____ (high, eloquent) about the government's plans, but he was _____ (rude) interrupted by the leader of the opposition.

14. There is no such thing as a _____ (moral) book or an _____ (immoral) book. Books are _____ (good) written or _____ (bad) written. That is all. (Oscar Wilde)

15. King's first book was an _____ (immense) success, and his second and third books have been _____ (enormous, successful) as well.

16. Diann was _____ (complete) devastated by her son's decision to leave home.

17. I was _____ (deep) shocked by the totally unexpected death of Rupert.

18. Ray speaks _____ (fluent) Italian and also speaks Spanish _____ (fluent).

19. The reviewer wrote _____ (enthusiastic) about J. K. Rowling's new book.

20. Power tends to corrupt, and absolute power corrupts _____ (absolute).

Test 49

ADVERBS

It is a universally acknowledged truth that a single man . . .  *. . . in possession of a fortune must be in need of a wife.*
— Jane Austen

FREQUENTLY ASKED QUESTIONS

Kombinieren Sie die Elemente aus den grauen Kästen und vervollständigen Sie die Sätze.

| A | **frequently** | hilariously | scientifically | seriously | strictly |
| B | carefully | diametrically | genetically | newly | wildly |

| A | **asked** | confidential | funny | ill | proven |
| B | guarded | married | modified | opposed | optimistic |

| A | comedian | document | fact | patient | **questions** |
| B | couple | food | outlook | secret | views |

A   1. Many websites have a section answering ____**frequently asked questions**____ (FAQs).

    2. It is a _____ that AIDS is caused by a virus.

    3. We were all laughing our heads off at the _____.

    4. It's a scandal that a _____ has to wait six months for an operation.

    5. Don't show this report to anybody, it is a _____.

B   6. Sixty per cent of Germans say they will never eat _____.

    7. Brenda and I can't agree on anything, we always have _____.

    8. The plans for the allied invasion in Normandy were a _____.

    9. On returning from their honeymoon the _____ bought a house.

    10. In a _____ the new manager talked of doubling the profits.

Test 50

So you want to be my son-in-law, young man?

Not exactly, I just want to marry your daughter.

SENTENCE ADVERBS

Die Adverbien der grauen Box bestimmen den gesamten Satzinhalt. Vervollständigen Sie die Sätze.

A

ironically	1. _____**Sadly**_____, Jim's operation hasn't improved his heart condition.
miraculously	2. The car was totally destroyed, but _____ the driver was unhurt.
personally	3. Al didn't prepare for his exam and, not _____, failed miserably.
sadly	4. _____, men who think they are the best drivers cause most accidents.
surprisingly	5. Foreign holidays are all very well, but _____ I prefer to stay in England.

B

absurdly	6. I thought Ben was working for his exam, but _____ he'd gone on holiday.
actually	7. Many kids are curious about drugs, but _____ our son won't touch them.
happily	8. _____, all cars should have passenger airbags.
ideally	9. _____, flying is much safer than driving a car.
statistically	10. _____, he blamed his wife for the fact that he had forgotten his keys.

C

foolishly	11. _____, the forest fire burnt itself out before it reached our village.
luckily	12. _____, the twins look exactly alike but it's quite easy to tell them apart.
obviously	13. _____, an asteroid might hit Earth but this is highly unlikely.
superficially	14. When we saw the car thieves we _____ rang the police.
theoretically	15. _____, Brian had left his map at home and couldn't find the way.

Test 51

ADVERBS

A CAREFUL DRIVER DRIVES CAREFULLY

Rewrite the sentences by using adverbs in place of the words in fat print.

1. Anne is a very **patient** listener. – __Anne listens patiently.__

2. Jean is a very **good** cook. – Jean cooks . . . _____

3. Bill gave a **happy** smile. – Bill . . . _____

4. Tobacco does **serious** damage to your health. – Tobacco . . . _____

5. They all looked at me with an **icy** stare. – They all . . . _____

6. I have a **full** explanation for everything. – I can . . . _____

7. There was an **immediate** reaction to our e-mails. – People . . . _____

8. Mum looked **with pride** at her daughter. – Mum . . . _____

9. The weather is cold, this is **unusual**. – The weather is . . . _____

10. What **irresponsible** behaviour! – How can he . . . _____

11. Susan completed her course **with success**. – Susan . . . _____

12. Vanessa is a **graceful** dancer. – Vanessa . . . _____

13. My uncle spoke in a **calm** way. – My uncle spoke . . . _____

14. King's new book was an **enormous** success. – King's new book . . . _____

15. I gave the house a **thorough** clean. – The house is now . . . _____

16. It is **clear** that your argument is absurd. – Your argument . . . _____

Test 52

REVISION · TRANSLATE

Adjektiv oder Adverb?

1. Wir öffneten vorsichtig die Tür.

2. Glücklicherweise ging Jims Operation gut.

3. Matt war schüchtern und lächelte nervös.

4. Die Kinder spielten glücklich und waren sehr laut.

5. Die Grünen wollen politisch korrekt sein.

6. Ich war angenehm überrascht von Alfreds Plan.

7. Emma begrüßte uns freundlich und hörte uns höflich zu.

8. George fährt extrem vorsichtig.

9. Es war ein heißer Tag, und wir gingen schnell zum Strand.

10. Hilary ist immer sehr elegant gekleidet.

11. Brian ist hochintelligent und extrem gut informiert.

12. In Spanien kannst du leicht ein Hotel finden.

13. Persönlich würde ich lieber in einem angenehm warmen Klima leben.

14. Diese Theorie ist wissenschaftlich bewiesen.

15. Bist du total verrückt? Du hast extrem unverantwortlich gehandelt.

ADVERBS

Test 53

*If you want my advice:
Whatever you do in life ...*
THINK BIG!

THINK BIG

Viele Adverbien haben die gleiche Form (ohne -ly) und weitgehend gleiche Bedeutung wie ihr Adjektiv. Vervollständigen Sie die Sätze mit den Adjektiven / Adverbien aus der grauen Box.

A	○ cheap	○ daily	○ deep	○ direct	○ early	○ **easy**
	○ fair	○ fast	○ free	○ late	○ right	○ wide
B	○ big	○ dear	○ extra	○ fine	○ flat	○ hard
	○ high	○ hourly	○ light	○ little	○ low	○ straight

ADJECTIVE | ADVERB

A

1. This is an ____**easy**____ problem to solve.   Don't worry too much! Take it ____**easy**____ !

2. I can only afford a _____ hotel.   I bought this carpet _____ in a sale.

3. The _____ movie starts at ten.   I apologised for arriving _____ .

4. _____ play is important in sports.   Please play _____ .

5. Mabel gave the _____ answer.   He's hopeless! He can't do anything _____ .

6. The Times is a _____ newspaper.   I meet my colleague Martin _____ .

7. He gave me a _____ smile.   I opened my mouth _____ for the dentist.

66

Test 53

8. Is this a _____ flight to Dallas?   We fly to Dallas _____.

9. The _____ bird gets the worm.   We arrived _____.

10. I have two _____ tickets for 'Cats'.   We didn't have to pay and got in _____.

11. There was a _____ hole in the road.   We had to dig _____ to find water.

12. Bolt Boyracer loves _____ cars.   Slow down, you're driving too _____.

B 13. We've had _____ weather all day.   We get along _____ with each other.

14. _____ clouds were hanging in the sky.   The swallows are flying very _____ today.

15. I wish I had a _____ stomach like you.   We lay _____ on the ground, enjoying the sun.

16. These _____ mountains are beautiful.   The plane flew _____ in the sky.

17. My _____ friend William has come.   This mistake will cost us _____.

18. This is a _____ problem.   Always think _____, and you'll succeed.

19. There is an _____ bus service to Rye.   The buses run _____, the next one is at two.

20. My parents had very _____ money.   I'm pretty tired, I slept very _____ last night.

21. Writing a poem can be _____ work.   We worked _____ to get the job done.

22. We'll wash your car at no _____ cost.   We had to pay _____ to get an upgrade.

23. My suitcase is very _____.   I always travel _____ rather than carry a case.

24. I need a ruler to draw a _____ line.   Please don't slouch and sit up _____.

Einige andere Adverbien haben ebenfalls die gleiche Form wie das Adjektiv, aber eine andere Bedeutung:

Latin is a **dead** language.   You have to drive **dead** slow here.
A **precious** pearl necklace . . .   I have **precious** little money.
A **sharp** knife . . .   Let's meet at two o'clock **sharp**.
Ted has a **low** voice.   Our funds are running **low**.
I put on a **clean** shirt.   I **clean** forgot Ann's birthday.

ADVERBS

Test 54

LOOKING GOOD – LINKING VERBS

Nicht jedes Adjektiv, das auf ein Verb folgt, wird zum Adverb. Vergleichen Sie:

Fay laughed **happily**.   Bezug auf das Verb, Aussage zu Art und Weise der Handlung   **ADVERB**

Fay felt **happy**.   Bezug auf das Subjekt, Aussage über Eigenschaft des Subjekts   **ADJEKTIV**

In „Fay felt happy" beschreibt **happy** nicht die Handlung des Fühlens, sondern das Satzsubjekt (Fay). Man spricht hier von Ergänzungen oder „Subjektkomplementen", die nach bestimmten Verben stehen: den **link verbs**. Diese stellen eine Verbindung (link) zwischen Subjekt und Ergänzung her. Kann ein Verb durch das klassische Link Verb **'to be'** (Fay felt happy → Fay was happy) ersetzt werden, handelt es sich um ein **link verb**, das mit Adjektiv steht.

Vervollständigen Sie die Sätze mit den Ergänzungen aus der grauen Box. (Keine Adverbformen verwenden!)

A

easy	1. The plane couldn't land and the passengers were growing ___**impatient**___.
empty	2. The railway line and the motorway follow the same route and run _____.
free	3. Suddenly Shorty went _____ with rage and started shouting and screaming.
frosty	4. We had expected a lot of traffic, but the roads proved _____.
impatient	5. Temperatures won't rise and the weather is going to stay _____.
parallel	6. Tom loves to be free, so having to follow orders won't come _____ to him.
true	7. Welcome to our house, please feel _____ to come and go as you want.
wild	8. For Harry a dream came _____ when Sally agreed to marry him.

B

calm	9. The door to Paul's house stood _____ and we just went in.
closed	10. At first Di was friendly, but then she turned _____ and shouted at me.
fat	11. The most important thing in case of a fire is not to panic and stay _____.
good	12. I like your new dress, you really look _____ in it.
nasty	13. Marlon used to be handsome, but then he gained weight and grew _____.
open	14. I'm pregnant, but please keep _____ and don't say a word to anybody.
quiet	15. Most banks in English provincial towns stay _____ on Saturdays.
terrible	16. The milk had turned sour and smelled _____.

Test 55

*You have the right to
remain silent . . . so please SHUT UP!*

SOUNDS GREAT!

Verbinden Sie die Linking Verbs aus der oberen Box mit den Adjektiven, um die Sätze zu vervollständigen.

A	get	grow	**remain**	smell	taste
B	feel	keep	seem	sound	stay
A	cold	damp	delicious	old	**silent**
B	calm	fit	happy	great	terrible

A 1. An arrested man has the right to ___**remain silent**___, but what he says can be used against him.

    2. It _____ very _____ in the desert once the sun has gone down.

    3. When you _____ your muscles get weaker and you lose your hair.

    4. We went down into the cellar, which was dark and wet and _____.

    5. Martha is a marvellous cook, her soups always _____.

B 6. I've had a nasty bout of flu for a week and I still _____.

    7. Don't get upset, try to _____.

    8. Swimming is a good sport, if you want to _____.

    9. Melanie _____; she was dancing around the room and singing loudly.

    10. The Maxines' new CD _____, it's really outstanding music.

ADVERBS

STELLUNG DER ADVERBIEN IM SATZ

Man occasionally stumbles over the truth, but most of the time he will pick himself up and continue on.

Für die Position der Adverbien im Satz gibt es oft mehrere Möglichkeiten, deren Wahl nicht nur von der inhaltlichen Bedeutung des Adverbs abhängt, sondern auch vom Bezug (auf welchen Satzteil bezieht sich das Adverb?) und den Sprechabsichten (was will der Sprecher betonen?).

Vor der Übertragung deutscher Muster ist zu warnen, was besonders für folgende Adverbien gilt:

Adverbien der unbestimmten Zeit:	now, soon, just, already, still
Adv. der unbestimmten Häufigkeit:	always, never, usually, normally, sometimes, rarely, occasionally
Adverbien der Wahrscheinlichkeit:	probably, definitely, certainly, presumably

Für die Stellung dieser Adverbien gelten folgende Regeln:

Vor dem Verb bei einfachen Verbformen:

I never forget my son's birthday.   Mark rarely missed a lesson.
James still lives in London.   Paul thoroughly enjoyed his stay in Paris.

Nach einfachen Formen von 'TO BE'

Zoe is always hungry after a swim.   We were always happy when we were young.
This author is certainly very interesting.   The child was probably an orphan.

Hat der Satz ein Hilfsverb oder mehrere Hilfsverben steht das Adverb nach dem ERSTEN Hilfsverb

Stevie may never be able to walk again.   Do you still live in California?
I will always love you.   Will doesn't usually drink wine.
Mary has really been working hard.   I will probably be seeing Janet this weekend.

Anders als im deutschen gilt: Kein Adverb zwischen Verb und Objekt

Nicht: *I go never to the theatre. / *Keith visits usually his parents on Sundays.*
Sondern: I never go to the theatre. / Keith usually visits his parents on Sundays.

Test 56

BESTIMMEN SIE DIE KORREKTE POSITION DES ADVERBS

1. I have been late for work. (never)
2. You can ask me. (always)
3. Phil will come tomorrow. (probably)
4. My mum's steaks are the best. (definitely)
5. March is the wettest month here. (usually)
6. Angela is quite generous. (normally)
7. You are right. (probably)
8. Theo has left the office. (already)
9. Al doesn't come here that early. (usually)
10. Eric has been ill this year. (frequently)
11. Bill has been drinking too much. (probably)
12. You must lie to me. (never)
13. Do you love me? (still)
14. We will go to Sue's party. (presumably)
15. I don't eat that late. (normally)
16. I have spoken to Anne. (just)
17. Our car has had to be repaired. (never)
18. I remember giving you the key. (definitely)

Test 57

ÜBERSETZEN SIE UNTER BESONDERER BEACHTUNG DER ADVERB-POSITION

1. Ich schlafe normalerweise sehr gut. _____
2. Leon ist gerade eben zurück gekommen. _____
3. Wir gehen oft ins Kino. _____
4. Sara ist wahrscheinlich nach Italien gefahren. _____
5. Lebt Eva noch in Brighton? _____
6. Ich habe das Auto schon gewaschen. _____
7. Ken hat (noch) nie ein Musical gesehen. _____
8. Kim wartet wahrscheinlich seit einer Stunde. _____
9. Ich trinke normalerweise kein Bier. _____
10. Martha arbeitet manchmal als Babysitter. _____
11. Dein neuer Job wird mit Sicherheit schwierig sein. _____
12. Dieser Schüler ist oft in America gewesen. _____

KEY

TEST YOUR GRAMMAR 5 · KEY

Evolution does not depend on the strongest or fastest organisms . . .

. . . but on the ones that are most adaptable.

Charles Darwin

TEST 1 — STEIGERN SIE DIE ADJEKTIVE — 11

awful	more awful	most awful	hot	hotter	hottest
busy	busier	busiest	impolite	more impolite	most impolite
cheap	cheaper	cheapest	intelligent	more intelligent	most intelligent
comfortable	more comfortable	most comfortable	many	more	most
deep	deeper	deepest	narrow	narrower	narrowest
distant	more distant	most distant	pretty	prettier	prettiest
dull	duller	dullest	quick	quicker	quickest
expensive	more expensive	most expensive	quiet	quieter	quietest
extreme	more extreme	most extreme	sad	sadder	saddest
famous	more famous	most famous	silly	sillier	silliest
fine	finer	finest	simple	simpler	simplest
free	freer	freest	solid	more solid	most solid
funny	funnier	funniest	strong	stronger	strongest
heavy	heavier	heaviest	terrible	more terrible	most terrible

TEST 2 — SUBSTANTIV → ADJEKTIV — 12

A	blood	bloody	B envy	envious	C order	orderly
	brother	brotherly	force	forceful	parliament	parliamentary
	centre	central	form	formal	poison	poisonous
	change	changeless	frost	frosty	profession	professional
	cost	costly	function	functional	rain	rainy
	coward	cowardly	ghost	ghostly	respect	respectful
	cream	creamy	glory	glorious	revolution	revolutionary
	dirt	dirty	legend	legendary	rock	rocky
	education	educational	luck	lucky	ruin	ruinous
	element	elementary	moment	momentary	scandal	scandalous
	emotion	emotional	neighbour	neighbourly	sun	sunny
	end	endless	night	nightly	year	yearly

KEY

TEST 3 — EVOLUTIONARY PROGRESS — 13

A
- regional accent
- childless couple
- global economy
- powerful engine
- environmental disaster

B
- sandy beach
- tactful diplomat
- musical instrument
- stressful job
- weekly magazine

C
- forceful personality
- evolutionary progress
- harmonious relationship
- dreamless sleep
- classless society

D
- mysterious stranger
- limitless supply
- clinical tests
- traditional values
- senseless violence

TEST 4 — WE ARE NOT AMUSED — 14

1. alarming
2. convincing
3. welcoming
4. overwhelming
5. threatening
6. challenging
7. distracting
8. amused
9. annoyed
10. refreshed
11. tempted
12. inspired
13. terrified
14. pleased

TEST 5 — USE THE CORRECT PARTICIPLES — 15

1. . . . is shrinking at an **alarming** rate.
2. Martha . . . got a **challenging** job in the City.
3. I don't find these arguments very **convincing** . . .
4. I find that very **distracting**.
5. Penny gave Ken a warm **welcoming** smile.
6. . . . won with an **overwhelming** majority.
7. The **threatening** behaviour of some . . .
8. . . . can keep her **amused** for hours.
9. Joan felt energetic and **refreshed** again.
10. My sister was **terrified** of walking home . . .
11. I felt **tempted** to have a piece of chocolate . . .
12. Many artists are **inspired** by the beauty . . .
13. Our parents were very **pleased** . . .
14. The passengers were very **annoyed** . . .

TEST 6 — WIT & WISDOM — 16

1. He who thinks himself **wise** . . . is a great fool.
2. How **wonderful** is that flash of a moment . . .
3. War does not determine who is **right** . . .
4. Nothing makes us so **lonely** as our secrets.
5. . . . **content** with little . . . **content** with much . .
6. No man is **useless** in this world . . .
7. Anyone can get **old**, all you have to do . . .
8. A **narrow** mind and a wide mouth . . .
9. We might all be **successful** if we . . .
10. Fifty-one per cent of being **smart** . . .
11. You can't be **brave**, if you only . . .
12. . . . the many who are **poor**, it can't . . .

KEY

Love is like war: easy to begin ... ... but very hard to stop.

Zsa Zsa Gabor

TEST 7   **OFFICE WISDOM**   **17**

1. If you're not **confused**, you're not ...
2. Only a **mediocre** person is always at his best.
3. No one is too **busy** to ... how **busy** he is.
4. Talk is **cheap** – until you hire a lawyer.
5. You're only **young** once ...
6. ... why aren't there more **happy** people?
7. ... one of them is **unnecessary**.
8. ... talking when one's head is **empty**?
9. You may be on the **right** track ...
10. **Honest** confession is good for the soul ...
11. Minds ... only work when they are **open**.
12. Make something **idiot-proof** and ...

We know our boss is efficient,
intelligent and kind - he told us so himself.

TEST 8   **BE BRIGHT-EYED AND BUSHY-TAILED**   **18**

A	full-bodied wine	C	fast-paced thriller
	hard-nosed businessman		full-throated laugh
	long-winded story		high-minded idealist
	single-minded determination		whole-hearted support
B	deep-rooted prejudices	D	far-sighted strategy
	foul-mouthed hooligan		high-powered car
	high-heeled shoes		one-sided view
	light-hearted comedy		short-sleeved shirt

TEST 9   **VERVOLLSTÄNDIGEN SIE DIE SÄTZE**   **19**

1. ... a **full-bodied wine** to go with our pasta ...
2. ... bore people with a **long-winded story**.
3. ... a **single-minded determination** to succeed.
4. A **hard-nosed businessman** like ...
5. **High-heeled shoes** look elegant ...
6. A **foul-mouthed hooligan** was shouting ...
7. ... fight against many **deep-rooted prejudices**.
8. 'Love in Funsville' is a **light-hearted comedy** ..
9. Rex gave a **full-throated laugh** ...
10. People with a **high-powered car** like ...
11. ... a **fast-paced thriller** with lots of car chases.
12. ... I'll give it my **whole-hearted support**.
13. Being a **high-minded idealist** is not enough ...
14. ... Bermuda shorts and a **short-sleeved shirt**.
15. Ron has an extremely **one-sided view** ...
16. ... what you need is a **far-sighted strategy**.

KEY

TEST 10 — HIGH-MINDED AND FAR-SIGHTED — 20

1. mean / hates spending — **tight-fisted**
2. easily excited — **hot-blooded**
3. young and healthy-looking — **fresh-faced**
4. needs plenty of time to understand — **slow-witted**
5. tolerant and liberal — **broad-minded**
6. If you easily get angry — **short-tempered**
7. indifferent to suffering — **hard-hearted**
8. insincere — **two-faced**
9. optimistic in a naive way — **starry-eyed**
10. refuses to talk — **tight-lipped**

TEST 11 — QUICK-WITTED SYNONYMS — 21

A
- absent-minded = forgetful
- big-headed = conceited
- big-hearted = generous
- blue-blooded = aristocratic
- cold-blooded = unfeeling
- cool-headed = rational

B
- even-handed = fair
- faint-hearted = cowardly
- flat-footed = clumsy

- high-spirited = lively
- high-principled = idealistic
- low-spirited = depressed

C
- mild-mannered = gentle
- muddle-headed = confused
- quick-witted = intelligent
- red-faced = embarrassed
- sure-footed = confident
- thick-skinned = insensitive

INFO 1 — WORD LIST

Weitere Adjektive nach dem Muster: ADJEKTIV + (SUBSTANTIV + -ed) = ADJEKTIV

ashen-faced	free-spirited	medium-sized	single-handed
bloody-minded	full-bodied wine	middle-aged	soft-hearted
broad-shouldered	good-hearted	narrow-minded	straight-faced
broken-hearted	good-tempered	nimble-footed	strong-boned
clear-sighted	grey-haired	old-fashioned	strong-minded
double-breasted suit	half-hearted attempt	one-armed bandit	strong-willed
empty-handed	high-pitched voice	open-minded	tender-hearted
even-tempered	kind-hearted	open-mouthed	warm-hearted
evil-minded terrorists	left-handed	red-blooded	weak-willed
flat-roofed building	light-fingered shoplifter	right-angled	white-haired
four-bedroomed flat	long-legged	rosy-cheeked child	wide-eyed
four-wheeled vehicle	loose-limbed	sharp-witted	
four-legged creature	low-pitched voice	silver-tongued charm	

KEY

TEST 12   **BE GRAMMAR-CONSCIOUS**   **22**

bullet-proof vest	job-related travel
child-proof lock	lead-free petrol
cliché-ridden political speech	meat-free diet
debt-ridden poor countries	oil-rich Gulf states
drug-related crime	oxygen-rich air
guilt-ridden neurotic	protein-rich nuts
health-conscious fitness trainer	rain-proof anorak
image-conscious movie star	safety-conscious security officer
interest-free loan	smoking-related cancer

TEST 13   **A BREATHTAKING EXERCISE**   **23**

A		B	
	labour-saving device		law-abiding citizen
	figure-hugging dress		mouth-watering desserts
	English-speaking nations		head-turning good looks
	ear-splitting noise		epoch-making event
	life-saving operation		breathtaking special effects

1. The washing machine is a **labour-saving device**
2. A **life-saving operation** like a heart by-pass . . .
3. . . . the **English-speaking nations** of . . .
4. In her **figure-hugging dress** actress . . .
5. . . . the **ear-splitting noise** of a rock concert . .
6. . . . was an **epoch-making event** . . .
7. . . . full of **breathtaking special effects** . . .
8. . . . their **mouth-watering desserts**.
9. No **law-abiding citizen** has anything to fear . .
10. . . . has **head-turning good looks**, he's . . .

WORD LIST   INFO 2

**Weitere Adjektive nach dem Muster: SUBSTANTIV + PRESENT PARTICIPLE (-ing) = ADJEKTIV
Zur Verdeutlichung werden passende Substantive mitgegeben.**

award-winning film	God-fearing people	soul-destroying job
back-breaking job	hair-raising mistake	spine-chilling horror movie
death-defying stunt	heart-breaking tragedy	thought-provoking article
energy-saving light bulbs	heart-warming love story	time-consuming routines
fund-raising campaign	ocean-going vessel	
gas-guzzling car	side-splitting laughter	

KEY

| **TEST 14** | | ACTION-PACKED AND TAILOR-MADE | | 24 |

A	B	C	D
action-packed film	calcium-enriched milk	gift-wrapped present	blood-stained shirt
alcohol-related accidents	hand-written letter	home-made soup	computer-aided design
air-conditioned hotel room	purpose-built flat	moth-eaten jacket	mass-produced souvenirs
tailor-made suit	star-studded show	snow-covered mountains	shark-infested waters
tree-lined avenue	state-owned industries	sun-drenched beaches	sugar-coated cake

| **TEST 15** | VERVOLLSTÄNDIGEN SIE DIE SÄTZE | 25 |

1. . . . an **action-packed film** . . .
2. . . . **tree-lined avenue** not far from the centre.
3. . . . return to my **air-conditioned hotel room**.
4. **Calcium-enriched milk** is supposed to . . .
5. . . . too many **alcohol-related accidents**.
6. . . . a **purpose-built flat** that exactly suits . . .
7. . . . in an elegant **tailor-made suit** . . .
8. The privatisation of **state-owned industries** . . .
9. . . . a **hand-written letter** makes . . .
10. 'Crazy' is a **star-studded show** . . .
11. . . . my grandmother's **home-made soup**.
12. Look at Sid's **blood-stained shirt**.
13. An old tramp in a **moth-eaten jacket** . . .
14. . . . a huge **gift-wrapped present**.
15. **Computer-aided design** is an important tool . .
16. Al's promises are like a **sugar-coated cake** . . .
17. . . . the **shark-infested waters** off the coast.
18. . . . terrible **mass-produced souvenirs**.
19. From the **snow-covered mountains** of the Sierra Nevada to the **sun-drenched beaches** . . .

| **INFO 3** | WORD LIST |

Weitere Adjektive nach dem Muster: SUBSTANTIV + PAST PARTICIPLE (-ed/3.Form) = ADJEKTIV
Zur Verdeutlichung werden passende Substantive mitgegeben.

army-controlled airport	graffiti-covered wall	rain-soaked walker
battle-scarred soldier	grief-stricken widow	rocket-propelled grenade (RPG)
book-lined library	hawk-eyed policeman	shop-soiled article
brain-damaged patient	home-grown vegetables	smoke-filled bar
child-centred learning	house-trained dog	strife-torn country
drug-crazed addict	learner-centred course	suntanned bathers
drug-related crime	life-sized wax figures	wheelchair-bound invalid
export-driven economy	London-based company	wind-blown streets
family-run business	Oxford-educated student	wood-panelled room
godforsaken place	panic-stricken child	
government-owned industry	poverty-stricken farmers	

Einige der Ajektive werden teilweise auch zusammengeschrieben; eine einheitliche Regel gibt es nicht.

KEY

TEST 16 — THE BIG-PRIZE TEST — 26

1. ... the ultimate **big-prize game show** of 2003.
2. ... on a **worst-case scenario**.
3. Our hospital needs an **intensive-care unit** ...
4. I'm afraid Al is just a **fair-weather friend** ...
5. We went to a **first-class restaurant** in Paris ...
6. Pain is the body's **early-warning system** ...
7. I'd like to see a proper **full-length feature film**.
8. ... a **high-risk investment** like shares ...
9. I hate **long-haul flights** ...
10. We booked an exclusive **five-star hotel** ...
11. ... a good **high-fidelity (hi-fi) sound system**.
12. ... the English have **hot-water bottles**.
13. I had watched a **late-night movie** ...
14. Without a **long-term solution** ...
15. Watch out, ... this is a **one-way street**.
16. A **free-market economy** will always be ...
17. A **multiple-choice test** gives you several answers
18. ... his **last-minute changes** to everything I do.

TEST 17 — A FIRST-CLASS HIGH-SPEED TEST — 27

1. ... fruit, nuts and **low-fat yoghurt**.
2. I only buy **free-range eggs**.
3. The Eurostar is a **high-speed train** ...
4. Travelling ... in a **hot-air balloon** ...
5. ... a **long-distance runner** from Kenya.
6. ... based on the **real-life experience** of ...
7. Marianne's is a typical **single-parent family** ...
8. It feels good to have a proper **full-time job** ...

WORD LIST — INFO 4

Weitere Adjektive nach dem Muster: ADJEKTIV + SUBSTANTIV = ADJEKTIV
Zur Verdeutlichung werden passende Substantive mitgegeben.

dead-end job	half-price offer	low-budget films
deep-sea fishing	high-definition television	low-level job
direct-mail campaign	high-class restaurant	low-risk investment
fast-food restaurant	high-level negotiations	modern-day life
fast-track career	high-profile celebrity	open-air concert
first-rate restaurant	human-rights campaigner	rapid-reaction force
first-hand knowledge	left-wing party	second-hand clothes / books
free-hand drawing	long-life milk	soft-top car
front-page news	long-range weather forecast	stainless-steel furniture
full-length dress	long-stay car park	strong-arm tactics
full-page advertisement	low-cost airline	top-level meeting

Einige der Ajektive – z.B. fast food restaurant, human rights campaigner – werden teilweise auch ohne Bindestrich (Hyphen) geschrieben; eine einheitliche Regel gibt es nicht.

KEY

TEST 18 **UP-TO-DATE INFORMATION** **28**

1. ... **up-to-date information** on ...
2. ... we offer **a round-the-clock-service.**
3. ... give **mouth-to-mouth resuscitation.**
4. Glen with his **happy-go-lucky attitude** ...
5. ... the **day-to-day running** of her boutique
6. I'm a practical **down-to-earth person.**
7. ... it was a **spur-of-the-moment decision.**
8. ... the support of its **rank-and-file members** ...
9. With their **head-in-the-sand attitude** ...
10. ... subtle **tongue-in-cheek humour.**
11. In a new **fly-on-the-wall documentary** ...
12. ... it's a typical **chicken-and-egg situation.**

TEST 19 **A STATE-OF-THE-ART TEST!** **29**

A
end-of-term school report
hit-and-run driver
nine-to-five job
on-the-spot fine
state-of-the-art technology
stop-and-go traffic

B
fun-in-the-sun holiday
middle-of-the-road politics
off-the-peg clothes
once-in-a-lifetime chance
rags-to-riches career
round-the-world cruise

1. With the very best **state-of-the-art technology** ...
2. ... are looking for the **hit-and-run driver** ...
3. In the **stop-and-go traffic** of the rush hour ...
4. ... his boring **nine-to-five job** in a bank.
5. ... pay an **on-the-spot fine** to ...
6. A pupil's **end-of-term school report** ...
7. ... we went on a **round-the-world cruise.**
8. ... sensible **middle-of-the-road politics** ...
9. I booked a **fun-in-the-sun holiday** in Spain.
10. In a typical **rags-to-riches career** ...
11. ... it's a **once-in-a-lifetime chance.**
12. I only wear **off-the-peg clothes.**

INFO 5 — WORD LIST

Das Englische macht von der Möglichkeit der adjektivischen Verwendung von Wortzusammensetzungen mit großem Erfindungsreichtum Gebrauch. Zur Verdeutlichung werden passende Substantive mitgegeben.

all-you-can-eat buffet	get-rich-quick scheme	once-in-a-lifetime holiday
bread-and-butter job	head-to-toe renovation	open-and-shut case
cash-and-carry supermarket	larger-than-life character	out-of-town supermarket
do-it-yourself store	law-and-order politics	over-the-counter drugs
door-to-door salesman	life-and-death matter	search-and-destroy mission
down-to-earth person	much-talked-about scandal	smash-and-grab raid
end-of-season sale	neck-and-neck race	touch-and-go situation
face-to-face discussion	never-to-be-forgotten experience	up-to-the-minute information

Je bekannter und verbreiteter die Ausdrücke sind, desto eher tendiert man zur Weglassung der ansonsten für das Verständnis notwendigen Bindestriche (die Übergänge sind hier fließend, und es gibt keine feste Regel).

bed and breakfast hotel	bread and butter job	fish and chip shop
black and white photograph	country and western music	drinking and driving offence

KEY

COLLOCATION • WORD PARTNERSHIPS

INFO 6

Dass man **Happy Christmas** und **Merry Christmas** aber nur **Happy Birthday** und nicht *Merry Birthday* sagt, ist keine Frage des Bedeutungsunterschiedes der Adjektive *merry* und *happy*, sondern eine der Kollokation: der „durch den Gebrauch der Sprache vorgegebenen Wortverbindungen" (Duden) und idiomatisierten Sprachkonvention. Diese ist nicht notwendigerweise „logisch" – und schon gar nicht aus der eigenen Muttersprache zu erschließen: **ein hoher Preis – a high price, ein hoher Turm – a tall tower; ein fester Preis – a fixed price, eine feste Freundschaft – a solid friendship, ein fester Händedruck – a firm handshake**.

Für dieses gewohnheitsmäßige und erwartbare gemeinsame Auftreten bestimmter Wörter hat das Englische auch den Begriff 'Word Partnerships'.

Ein solider Wortschatz ist deshalb nicht über isolierte Vokabelheft-Einträge zu erreichen, sondern nur über das Wissen um die idiomatisch korrekten Verbindungen, die das jeweilige Wort mit anderen Wörtern eingehen kann. „Auch die Lexik (Wortschatz) hat so eine Tiefenstruktur. Das aber bedeutet: **Auch in der Lexik wird innerhalb der Wortgrenze Grammatik wirksam.**" (W. Steinbrecht. Alles Literacy? Gymnasium in Niedersachsen 1/04)

TEST 20 — COOL COLLOCATIONS — 30

1. ... drive carefully and have a **safe journey**.
2. ... a **major factor** in the spread of AIDS.
3. It was a **steep climb** up the cliffs ...
4. **Tropical rain forests** are home to ...
5. ... the **freezing temperatures** of Alaska.
6. ... the most well-known **female novelist** ...
7. I want to go back to a **regular income** again.
8. Without the **solid support** of his party ...
9. I have a **vague memory** of the accident ...
10. Shakespeare with his **extensive vocabulary** ...
11. ... most dangerous **poisonous snakes**.
12. ... they had a **spectacular fireworks** display.
13. ... a **peaceful demonstration** ...
14. Marlon ... had to pay a **hefty fine**.
15. ... based on a **true story** from World War II.
16. I don't want to make a **wrong decision** ...

TEST 21 — ADJECTIVE & NOUN PARTNERSHIPS — 31

A
curly hair
general election
global economy
high season
humble apology

B
gradual development
illegal drugs
industrial revolution
instinctive reaction
sandy beach

C
gentle breeze
professional footballer
new-born baby
hearty welcome
totalitarian state

D
brutal murder
intensive care
keen intellect
logical conclusion
nervous breakdown

E
cancerous tumour
fair play
geometric pattern
loyal supporter
moral standard

F
boundless energy
first-class ticket
foreseeable future
fragrant perfume
solid foundation

KEY

TEST 22 — CHOOSE THE CORRECT ADJECTIVE — 32

1. These shoes are too **tight**.
2. ... but it was a **false** alarm.
3. The **final** decision rests with Mr Bigboss.
4. It is my **firm** belief that Sue is right.
5. This watch is made of **solid** gold.
6. The **rough** sea caused the ship to sink.
7. I learnt to ski on a **gentle** slope in the Alps.
8. What you say is a **gross** exaggeration.
9. The **harsh** truth is that Sam lied to you.
10. Mark is in bed with a **heavy** cold.
11. This cooking oil is of **poor** quality.
12. The planet Mars is visible to the **naked** eye.
13. In Spain it is **common** practice to stay up late.
14. The accident caused **serious** damage to my car.

TEST 23 — CHOOSE THE CORRECT ADJECTIVE — 33

1. Blub should go on a diet, he's much too **fat**.
2. Thank you for your **prompt** reply to our letter.
3. Without **electric** guitars there ...
4. Ray is a **handsome** man.
5. We had a very **lively** conversation about art.
6. I love my aunt's **tasty** potato soup.
7. Never dive into the **shallow** end ...
8. We offer a **wide** choice of flavours.
9. That was a very **fruitful** discussion.
10. Barry needed **medical** treatment.
11. To my **immense** relief Kim survived her illness.
12. It is a **great** honour to meet you.
13. There is a **close** connection between ...
14. Paul died in a **fatal** accident on the M1.
15. There is a **remote** chance that ...
16. Drinking causes **permanent** damage ...
17. Driving is fun on the **wide** roads of America.
18. The officer took a **quick** look at my passport.
19. We cycled down a **narrow** lane.
20. **Heavy** rain caused flooding on the roads.

TEST 24 — COLLOCATION TRIOS • 1 — 34

A
high .... expectations ..... standards ..... speed
intensive ... care .... farming .... course
massive .... heart attack .... debts .... increase

great .... honour .... tragedy .... pleasure
local .... telephone call .. newspaper ... time
hot .... competition ...... food .... favourite

B
narrow ..... road .... outlook .... victory
low .... price .... season .... quality
powerful .. car .... country .... drug

serious ..... doubt .... problem .... talk
sharp .... intellect .... knife .... contrast
accurate ... description ..... diagnosis ..... prediction

TEST 25 — COLLOCATION TRIOS • 2 — 35

fresh .... food .... evidence ...... air
ancient ..... monument ...... legend .... history
bitter .... quarrel .... remorse .... taste
broad .... consensus ...... smile .... accent
hearty ...... laugh .... meal .... welcome
personal .. computer .... belongings ... friend

deep .... gratitude .... shock .... snow
close .... connection .... friend .... resemblance
clear .... sky .... eyes .... voice
diplomatic .. relations .... service .... immunity
wide .... variety .... street .... gap
private .... enterprise ..... detective .... school

82

KEY

FIXED PAIRS — INFO 7

Unter **Fixed Pairs** versteht man feststehende Kombinationen aus Adjektiv und Substantiv, die sich zu eigenen neuen Ausdrücken verfestigt haben, wie ein selbständiges Wort funktionieren und deshalb auch in guten Wörterbüchern als eigene Einträge aufgeführt werden.

Das attributiv-bestimmende Adjektiv hat in Fixed Pairs seine Selbständigkeit verloren und ist fest mit dem Ausdruck verwachsen. Es kann deshalb auch nicht wie ein 'freies Adjektiv' gesteigert werden:

a political party / **Nicht:** *a more political party*   a fixed idea / **Nicht:** *a more fixed idea*

TEST 26 — FIND THE HAPPY MEDIUM — 36

1. ... is a **happy medium**.
2. ... two children from a **previous marriage**.
3. Amy and Joan are **identical twins** ...
4. You should take **professional advice** ...
5. ... start **primary school** when they are five.
6. ... largest inhabited **royal palace** in the world.
7. ... if I can give him some **moral support**.
8. ... **racial prejudice** against black people.
9. ... the **final decision** lies with my boss.
10. ... and **social mobility** is the norm.

TEST 27 — ADJECTIVE & NOUN • FIXED PAIRS — 37

A
- Endphase – final stage
- Flutwelle – tidal wave
- Grundlohn – basic wages
- Haushaltshilfe – domestic help
- Jugendkriminalität – juvenile delinquency
- Monatsmagazin – monthly magazine
- Schutzkleidung – protective clothing
- Verfassungsgericht – constitutional court
- Verhaltenstherapie – occupational therapy

B
- Außenpolitik – foreign policy
- Gentechnik – genetical engineering
- Geschlechtskrankheit – venereal disease
- Jahresurlaub – annual holiday
- Justizirrtum – judicial error
- Musikinstrument – musical instrument
- Parlamentswahl – parliamentary election
- Sonnenenergie – solar energy
- Vorzugsbehandlung – preferential treatment

WORD LIST — INFO 8

Deutsch: Nominalzusammensetzung = Englisch: Adjektiv + Substantiv

atomic energy	elementary school	lunar landscape	parliamentary elections
aquatic bird	facial expression	male choir	professional soldier
basic law	federal government	medical student	remedial tuition
civil war	foreign minister	mental illness	rural population
coastal town	global economy	monetary union	structural reform
cultural heritage	honorary member	monthly wages	toxic waste
domestic flight	industrial estate	natural disaster	urban planning
economic growth	local time	nocturnal animal	violent crime

KEY

TEST 28 — WITH FLYING COLOURS — 38

1. Vanessa passed her exam with **flying colours** . .
2. . . . it was just a **passing fancy**.
3. Life under the Taliban . . . was a **living hell**.
4. Winning the Nobel prize is the **crowning glory**
5. . . . put the **finishing touches** to it.
6. . . . it's a **standing joke**.
7. Papa was a **rolling stone** . . .
8. A woman is often the actual **driving force** . . .
9. Beryl bought a **matching pair** of vases . . .
10. . . . we had to walk through the **pouring rain**.
11. . . . you see that he was a **raving lunatic**.
12. Mother Teresa was a **shining example** . . .
13. . . . they had a **blazing row** over money.
14. . . . with a **gaping wound** in his left leg.
15. As a **practising doctor** I just . . .
16. . . . Paul is the new **rising star** of the art world.

TEST 29 — LIVING PROOF — 39

A
burning ambition   paying guest
living proof   roaring success
opposing views   standing invitation

B
deafening noise   living creatures
developing countries striking similarity
flying start   winning team

1. Bill Gates is **living proof** of the fact that . . .
2. . . . a **burning ambition** to win Wimbledon.
3. The new musical is a **roaring success** . . .
4. . . . stay in private homes as a **paying guest**.
5. . . . you know you have a **standing invitation**.
6. Stella and John have **opposing views** . . .
7. **Developing countries** can only prosper. . .
8. . . . all other **living creatures** . . .
9. 'Never change a **winning team**' . . .
10. Ken has got off to a **flying start** . . .
11. . . . Sue bears a **striking similarity** to . . .
12. . . . the **deafening noise** of a low-flying plane.

TEST 30 — MIXED BAG — 40

1. The visitors were a **mixed bag** . . .
2. **Organised crime** is one of . . .
3. . . . a case of **mistaken identity** . . .
4. Hotels with a **licensed bar** . . .
5. . . . I live in **rented accommodation**.
6. . . . homeless person . . . 'of no **fixed abode**'.
7. Joan spoke in a **hushed voice** . . .
8. . . . the most popular **stringed instrument** . .
9. 'Bobby' . . . an English **uniformed policeman**.
10. . . . always employ a **skilled craftsman**.
11. I'm quite happy with a cheap **used car**.
12. A copy of a special **limited edition** . . .
13. I have **mixed feelings** about emigrating.
14. . . . she is an exceptionally **gifted child**.

TEST 31 — MAKE A CONCENTRATED EFFORT — 41

1. concentrated effort
2. pointed remark
3. broken home
4. registered letter
5. furnished apartment
6. scheduled flight
7. packed lunch
8. armed forces
9. mixed blessing
10. hired hand
11. charmed life
12. extended family

KEY

TEST 32 — ADJECTIVE SYNONYMS — 42

A
- accurate – precise
- bizarre – weird
- clumsy – awkward
- cosy – comfortable
- creative – original
- distant – remote

B
- genuine – real
- ghastly – grim
- loud – noisy
- lucky – fortunate
- miserable – unhappy
- naked – nude

C
- lazy – idle
- modest – humble
- precious – valuable
- simple – elementary
- strong – powerful
- tasty – delicious

D
- curious – nosy
- exhausted – tired
- honest – truthful
- perfect – ideal
- stubborn – obstinate
- tactful – considerate

TEST 33 — COOL, CALM AND COLLECTED — 43

A
- able .... competent .... efficient
- clever .... brainy .... intelligent
- cool .... calm .... collected
- correct .... appropriate .... right
- dull .... boring .... tedious
- enthusiastic .... eager .... keen

B
- elegant .... fashionable .... stylish
- famous .... renowned .... well-known
- friendly .... helpful .... sociable
- neat .... orderly .... tidy
- rich .... affluent .... wealthy
- wild .... fierce .... savage

TEST 34 — ODD ONE OUT — 44

1. cosy .... comfortable ..... *harsh .. snug
2. faint .... feeble .... weak ..... *unhappy
3. brutal .... sadistic .... nasty ..... *proper
4. kind .... good-natured ... *tired ... thoughtful
5. *lucky ..... happy .... glad ...... cheerful
6. *cheap ... idle .... lazy ...... sluggish
7. silly .... foolish .... stupid .... *serious
8. *careless . lively .... quick ..... alert
9. precise ..... *tasteful .... exact ..... correct
10. pure .... *expensive ... clean .... spotless
11. *delicious ... false .... incorrect .. wrong
12. sad .... unhappy ..... *content .. miserable
13. fit .... *helpful ...... healthy .... sound
14. dull .... *strong ...... boring ..... tiresome
15. curious .... prying .... nosy .... *generous
16. modest .... *crazy .... humble ... shy
17. massive .... *dangerous huge .... enormous
18. unusual .... *dirty .... rare .... infrequent

85

KEY

TEST 35 — **A PLEASANT / AGREEABLE TEST** — 45

1. . . . a very **pleasant** / **agreeable** afternoon. . .
2. . . . a very **well-behaved** / **polite** young lady. .
3. We need a **permanent** / **lasting** solution . . .
4. . . . much more **rigid** / **inflexible** than . . .
5. It was quite **plain** / **obvious** to the police . . .
6. . . . behave like an **adult** / a **grown-up** person.
7. The **continuous** / **ceaseless** roar . . .
8. At some **remote** / **distant** time in the future . . .
9. . . . **basic** / **fundamental** rights in a democracy.
10. Martha is the **ideal** / **perfect** wife for Mark . . .
11. Honesty is a **stable** / **solid** foundation . . .
12. Marco's **arrogant** / **conceited** belief that. . .
13. My aunt . . . leads a very **busy** / **active** life.
14. . . . the **sacred** / **holy** shrine of the tiger god.

TEST 36 — **DEAD OR ALIVE • ADJECTIVE ANTONYMS** — 46

A
- alive – dead
- early – late
- empty – full
- fast – slow
- low – high
- rare – common

B
- bright – dark
- calm – nervous
- cheap – expensive
- clean – dirty
- concrete – abstract
- harmless – dangerous

C
- guilty – innocent
- hard – soft
- heavy – light
- mean – generous
- short – long
- similar – different

D
- idle – busy
- nice – nasty
- simple – complicated
- single – married
- wasteful – economical
- wise – foolish

*It's the good girls who keep a diary,
the bad girls never have the time.*

TEST 37 — **MORE ANTONYMS** — 47

a tame animal ⟺ a wild animal
stale bread ⟺ fresh bread
an alcoholic drink ⟺ a soft drink
an electric guitar ⟺ an acoustic guitar
ancient history ⟺ modern history
a sharp knife ⟺ a blunt knife

natural light ⟺ artificial light
a wide road ⟺ a narrow road
a permanent solution ⟺ a temporary solution
an amusing story ⟺ a boring story
an easy task ⟺ a difficult task
a tall man ⟺ a short man

KEY

TEST 38 **FIND THE ANTONYM PAIRS** 48

1. full – empty
2. rough – smooth
3. strong – weak
4. shallow – deep
5. hungry – full
6. arrogant – humble
7. polite – rude
8. quiet – noisy
9. tiny – huge
10. clumsy – skilful
11. serious – funny
12. sweet – sour
13. absent – present
14. strange – familiar
15. common – rare
16. kind – malicious
17. wealthy – poor
18. loose – tight

TEST 39 **FIND TWO ANTONYMS** 49

calm ⟺ frantic .... wild
cheerful ⟺ depressed ..... sad
clear ⟺ obscure .... vague
dangerous ⟺ safe .... secure
deceitful ⟺ honest .... trustworthy
dry ⟺ damp .... wet

easy ⟺ difficult .... hard
faulty ⟺ flawless .... perfect
quiet ⟺ loud .... noisy
reluctant ⟺ eager .... keen
sick ⟺ healthy .... well
unimportant ⟺ essential .... relevant

TEST 40 **A TEST FOR THE INTELLIGENT** 50

1. . . . a playgound of the **rich** and the **famous**
2. . . . so that **the blind** know when to cross . . .
3. . . . trained to give first aid to **the injured**.
4. When the rich make war it's **the poor** that die.
5. . . . available to **the homeless**.
6. The innocent and **the beautiful** have . . .
7. . . . create jobs for **the unemployed**.
8. . . . moved into a home for **the elderly**.
9. . . . enough noise to wake up **the dead**.
10. . . . she's lucky she's still among **the living**.
11. . . . working with **the young** is never boring.
12. . . . feed **the hungry** . . . hospitals for **the sick**.

TEST 41 **MAY THE BEST PERSON WIN** 51

1. The most important thing is that we are happy.
2. Money is the only thing I need.
3. Overweight people often have diabetes.
4. The most beautiful thing in life is love.
5. The good thing about Susan is her reliability.
6. The whole thing is a lie.
7. A rich man / person has no problems.
8. A sick or handicapped person needs help.
9. May the best man / woman win!
10. A dead man / person deserves respect.
11. We must not sentence an innocent person.
12. M. helped a blind man / person across the road.

KEY

INFO 9 — ADJEKTIVE ALS SUBSTANTIVE

You must excuse Herbert, he's trying to think the unthinkable

In geringerem Umfang können substantivierte Adjektive auch für abstrakte Begriffe verwendet werden.

Rechne immer mit **dem Unerwarteten**.	Always expect **the unexpected**.
Freuds Theorie **des Unbewussten** ist richtig.	Freud's theory of **the unconscious** is correct.
Niemand kann **Unmögliches** von dir verlangen.	Nobody can ask you to do **the impossible**.
Dies ist eine Mischung aus **Altem** und **Neuem**.	This is a mixture of **the old** and **the new**.
Das **Schlimmste** ist vorbei. Hoffen wir das **Beste**.	**The worst** is over. Let's hope for **the best**.
Unser Sohn fürchtet sich im **Dunklen**.	Our son is afraid of **the dark**.

TEST 42 — ANALYSE THIS TEST CLOSELY! — 54

1. The audience . . . **applauded wildly** at . . .
2. Good investors **analyse** the market **closely** . . .
3. Sheila . . . **greeted** me **warmly** with a hug.
4. . . . I **totally disagree** with you there.
5. Tobacco **seriously damages** your health.
6. Paul **accidentally tripped** over a stone and fell.
7. Annie can . . . **easily afford** a new car.
8. . . . I **took** it **gently** out of the box.
9. Mrs Summer **arranged** the flowers **prettily** . . .
10. It was **constantly raining** on our holiday . . .
11. The police **falsely accused** Jim of theft . . .
12. . . . we **confidently expect** to win this match.
13. . . . I can **fully explain** everything.
14. I would **strongly recommend** you to read . . .
15. Roy . . . **quickly withdrew**.
16. **Sitting correctly** greatly reduces tiredness . . .

TEST 43 — ADVERB & VERB PARTNERSHIPS — 55

1. I **remember vividly** how Terry had a row . . .
2. The students . . . **listened attentively**.
3. . . . **clashed violently** with the police.
4. The children **laughed happily** when . . .
5. . . . always **travel separately** in case . . .
6. . . . please **give generously**.
7. The audience **watched curiously** as . . .
8. . . . we **arrived safely** at my sister's house.
9. '**Speak softly** and carry a big stick' . . .
10. The ballerina **danced gracefully** . . .

KEY

| TEST 44 | FOR HIGHLY INTELLIGENT PEOPLE ONLY | 56 |

1. As an **immensely successful** businessman . . .
2. . . . famous for its **cleverly written** articles.
3. . . . everything is so **boringly familiar**.
4. . . . we only serve **locally caught** fish . . .
5. . . . everything was so **excitingly new**.
6. I was **pleasantly surprised** when . . .
7. Kate's daughter is **highly intelligent** . . .
8. . . . the sea was **perfectly calm**.
9. . . . I'm **absolutely convinced** of it.
10. It was **utterly irresponsible** of Dan to . . .
11. . . . the most **densely populated** places . . .
12. Mustique is a **privately owned** island . . .
13. It is not considered **politically correct** to . . .
14. The new film is **extremely popular**.
15. James became almost **totally blind** . . .
16. . . . her kitchen is always **spotlessly clean**.
17. . . . was to be **brutally honest**.
18. I am **heavily indebted** to you for . . .

| TEST 45 | CLEARLY VISIBLE WORD PARTNERSHIPS | 57 |

1. Mars is **clearly visible** to the naked . . .
2. Ben suddenly became **acutely aware** of . . .
3. What a **hideously ugly** building!
4. . . . is **vitally important** for the survival . . .
5. . . . by the **dazzlingly bright** sunshine . . .
6. Only **genuinely interested** customers . . .
7. . . . even the kids were **grossly overweight**.
8. . . . have a **carefully planned** strategy.
9. My father was **scrupulously honest**.
10. . . . with their **richly decorated** interiors.

Before God we are all equally wise . . . . . . and equally foolish.   Einstein

| TEST 46 | ABSOLUTELY CORRECT | 58 |

A
elegantly dressed
ideally suited
slightly damaged
strikingly beautiful
wholeheartedly committed

B
deadly serious
eternally grateful
fatally injured
radically different
theoretically possible

1. . . . important to be **elegantly dressed** . . .
2. . . . was **wholeheartedly committed** to . . .
3. Ned . . . is **ideally suited** to the job.
4. The table was **slightly damaged** . . .
5. Di looked so **strikingly beautiful** . . .
6. . . . **radically different** to the war-torn . . .
7. It is **theoretically possible** but highly unlikely. . .
8. The accident victim was **fatally injured** . . .
9. The US is always **deadly serious** when . . .
10. . . . I'll be **eternally grateful** to you.

KEY

| TEST 47 | ADVERB & ADJECTIVE PARTNERSHIPS | 59 |

entfernt verwandt – distantly related
geistig behindert – mentally handicapped
glücklich verheiratet – happily married
hochintelligent – highly intelligent
maßlos übertrieben – grossly exaggerated
schlecht bezahlt – badly paid
sorgfältig geplant – carefully planned
unheilbar krank – terminally ill
voll möbliert (Wohnung) – fully furnished
wissenschaftlich bewiesen – scientifically proven

demokratisch gewählt – democratically elected
frisch gemahlen (Kaffee) – freshly ground
gut informiert – well informed
hochqualifiziert – highly qualified
körperlich gesund – physically fit
umweltfreundlich – environmentally friendly
voll funktionsfähig – fully operational
weitgereist – widely travelled
zutiefst besorgt – deeply worried
zutiefst verschieden – fundamentally different

| TEST 48 | ADJECTIVE or ADVERB? | 60 |

1. It's better to travel **hopefully** than to arrive.
2. ... were **graceful** as she moved **extremely slowly** around ... a very **attractive** woman.
3. ... we **quickly** went inside.
4. It is **morally** wrong to lie to people ...
5. ... **good** at ... speaks English very **well**, too.
6. ... a **beautifully** shaped face and **shiny** hair.
7. ... **deeply** in love, ... **truly** made for each other, ... **sunny** day ... **happily** ever after.
8. ... **badly** ventilated ... some **fresh** air.
9. ... stands **majestically** at the end of the Mall.
10. ... developed **specifically** for teenagers.
11. ... are both **extremely successful** solicitors.
12. ... **frightfully** wet, I felt **miserable** and cold.
13. ... **highly eloquently** ... **rudely** interrupted
14. ... as a **moral** book or an **immoral** book. Books are **well** written or **badly** written.
15. ... an **immense** success, his second and third book have been **enormously successful** ...
16. Diann was **completely** devastated by ...
17. I was **deeply** shocked by ...
18. ... **fluent** Italian. ... speaks Spanish **fluently**.
19. The reviewer wrote **enthusiastically** about ...
20. ... absolute power corrupts **absolutely**.

| TEST 49 | FREQUENTLY ASKED QUESTIONS | 62 |

1. ... answering **frequently asked questions** ...
2. It is a **scientifically proven fact** that ...
3. ... at the **hilariously funny comedian**.
4. It's a scandal that a **seriously ill patient** ...
5. ... it is **a strictly confidential document**.
6. ... will never eat **genetically modified food**.
7. ... always have **diametrically opposed views**.
8. The plans ... were a **carefully guarded secret**.
9. ... he **newly married couple** bought a house.
10. In a **wildly optimistic outlook** the ...

KEY

A person who loses his head . . . 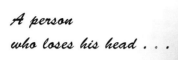 *. . . usually is the last one to miss it.*

TEST 50   **SENTENCE ADVERBS**   **63**

1. **Sadly**, Jim's operation hasn't improved . . .
2. . . . but **miraculously** the driver was unhurt.
3. . . . **not surprisingly**, failed miserably.
4. **Ironically**, men who think . . .
5. . . . **personally** I prefer to stay in England.
6. . . . but **actually** he'd gone on holiday.
7. . . . **happily** our son won't touch them.
8. **Ideally**, all cars should have passenger airbags.
9. **Statistically**, flying is much safer . . .
10. **Absurdly**, he blamed his wife for . . .
11. **Luckily** the forest fire burnt itself out . . .
12. **Superficially**, the twins look exactly alike, . . .
13. **Theoretically**, an asteroid might hit Earth . . .
14. . . . we **obviously** rang the police.
15. **Foolishly**, Brian had left his map . . .

SATZADVERBIEN ALS KURZANTWORT   INFO 10

Satzadverbien werden auch als Kurzantworten in Reaktion auf einen gesamten Satz verwendet.

Linda's back from Japan. – Oh, **really**? I thought she was coming next week.
Would you like to go on a luxury cruise? – **Definitely**.
Would you like a room with sea views? – **Preferably** yes.
So you left James when you found him cheating on you? – **Naturally**.

TEST 51   **A CAREFUL DRIVER DRIVES CAREFULLY**   **64**

1. Anne listens **patiently**.
2. Jean cooks very **well**.
3. Bill smiled **happily**.
4. Tobacco **seriously** damages your health.
5. They all stared at me **icily**.
6. I can **fully** explain everything.
7. People reacted **immediately** to our e-mails.
8. Mum looked **proudly** at her daughter.
9. The weather is **unusually** cold.
10. How can he behave so **irresponsibly**!
11. Susan **successfully** completed her course.
12. Vanessa dances **gracefully**.
13. My uncle spoke **calmly**.
14. King's new book was **enormously** successful.
15. The house is now **thoroughly** clean.
16. Your argument is **clearly** absurd.

KEY

TEST 52 — REVISION • TRANSLATE — 65

1. We opened the door carefully. / We carefully opened the door.
2. Luckily/Fortunately Jim's operation went well.
3. Matt was shy and smiled nervously.
4. The children played happily and were very noisy.
5. The Greens want to be politically correct.
6. I was pleasantly surprised by Alfred's plan.
7. Emma greeted us in a friendly way and listened to us politely.
8. George drives extremely carefully.
9. It was a hot day and we quickly went to the beach.
10. Hilary is always very elegantly dressed.
11. Brian is highly intelligent and extremely well informed.
12. In Spain you can easily find a hotel.
13. Personally, I'd rather live in a pleasantly warm climate.
14. This theory is scientifically proven.
15. Are you totally crazy? You have acted extremely irresponsibly.

TEST 53 — THINK BIG — 66

ADJECTIVE	ADVERB	ADJECTIVE	ADVERB
1. . . . **easy** problem.	Take it **easy**!	13. . . . **fine** weather.	We get along **fine** . . .
2. . . . a **cheap** hotel.	I bought this carpet **cheap**.	14. **Low** clouds . . .	. . . flying very **low** today.
3. The **late** movie . . .	. . . arriving **late**.	15. . . . a **flat** stomach.	We lay **flat** on the ground.
4. **Fair** play . . .	Please play **fair**.	16. . . . **high** mountains.	The plane flew **high** . . .
5. . . . the **right** answer.	. . . do anything **right**.	17. My **dear** friend . . .	. . . will cost us **dear**.
6. . . . **daily** newspaper.	I meet Martin **daily**.	18. . . . a **big** problem.	Always think **big** . . .
7. . . . a **wide** smile.	. . . my mouth **wide** . . .	19. . . . **hourly** service.	The buses run **hourly** . . .
8. . . . a **direct** flight.	We fly to Dallas **direct**.	20. . . . very **little** money.	. . . I slept very **little** . . .
9. The **early** bird . . .	We arrived **early**.	21. . . . **hard** work.	We worked **hard** . . .
10. . . . two **free** tickets.	. . . got in **free**.	22. . . . at no **extra** cost.	We had to pay **extra** . . .
11. . . . a **deep** hole . . .	We had to dig **deep**.	23. . . . is very **light**.	I always travel **light** . . .
12. . . . loves **fast** cars.	. . . driving too **fast**.	24. . . . a **straight** line.	. . . sit up **straight**.

TEST 54 — LOOKING GOOD - LINKING VERBS — 68

Zur Information sind die Link Verbs ebenfalls fett gedruckt.

1. . . . the passengers were **growing impatient**.
2. The railway line and the motorway **run parallel**.
3. Suddenly Shorty **went wild** with rage . . .
4. . . . but the roads **proved empty**.
5. . . . the weather is going to **stay frosty**.
6. . . . to follow orders won't **come easy** to him.
7. . . . please **feel free** to come and go . . .
8. For Harry a dream **came true** when Sally . . .
9. The door to Paul's house **stood open** . . .
10. . . . she **turned nasty** and shouted at me.
11. The most important thing is to **stay calm**.
12. . . . you really **look good** in it.
13. . . . he gained weight and **grew fat**.
14. I'm pregnant, but please **keep quiet** . . .
15. . . . **stay closed** on Saturdays.
16. The milk . . . **smelled terrible**.

KEY

TEST 55   **SOUNDS GREAT!**   69

1. . . . has the right to **remain silent** . . .
2. It **gets very cold** in the desert . . .
3. When you **grow old** your muscles get weaker . .
4. . . . which was dark and wet and **smelled damp**.
5. . . . her soups always **taste delicious**.
6. . . . I still **feel terrible**.
7. Don't get upset, try to **stay calm**.
8. . . . if you want to **keep fit**.
9. Melanie **seemed happy**; she was dancing . . .
10. The Maxines' new CD **sounds great** . . .

TEST 56   **BESTIMMEN SIE DIE KORREKTE POSITION DES ADVERBS**   71

1. I have **never** been late for work.
2. You can **always** ask me.
3. Phil will **probably** come tomorrow.
4. My mum's steaks are **definitely** the best.
5. March is **usually** the wettest month here.
6. Angela is **normally** quite generous.
7. You are **probably** right.
8. Theo has **already** left the office.
9. Al doesn't **usually** come here that early.
10. Eric has **frequently** been ill this year.
11. Bill has **probably** been drinking too much.
12. You must **never** lie to me.
13. Do you **still** love me?
14. We will **presumably** go to Sue's party.
15. I don't **normally** eat that late.
16. I have **just** spoken to Anne.
17. Our car has **never** had to be repaired.
18. I **definitely** remember giving you the key.

Now, look. I didn't come here to be insulted.

Oh, really? Where do you usually go?

TEST 57   **ÜBERSETZUNG**   71

1. I **normally** sleep very well.
2. Leon has **just** come back.
3. We **often** go to the cinema.
4. Sara has **presumably/probably** gone to Italy.
5. Does Eva **still** live in Brighton?
   oder: Is Eva **still** living in Brighton?
6. I have **already** washed the car.
7. Ken has **never** seen a musical.
8. Kim has **probably** been waiting for an hour by now.
9. I don't **normally** drink beer.
10. Martha **sometimes** works as a babysitter.
11. Your new job will **definitely** be difficult / is **definitely** going to be difficult.
12. This student has **often** been to America.

BEAVER BOOKS

TEST YOUR GRAMMAR

Vier weitere Bände von **TEST YOUR GRAMMAR** sind erhältlich. Jeder Band hat 96 Seiten mit zahlreichen Illustrationen und Cartoons sowie einem ausführlichen Key mit Lösungen, Zusatzinformationen und Word Lists.

❶ NOUNS · SUBSTANTIVE

- Collective Nouns
- Plural Nouns
- Deutsch-englische Unterschiede im Gebrauch von Singular und Plural
- Unterschiede im Artikelgebrauch
- of-Genitiv und Apostroph-Genitiv
- Zählbare & nicht-zählbare Substantive
- Partitive Strukturen
- Wortbildung: Compound Nouns
- Die „beliebtesten" Fehler der Deutschen

❷ PRONOUNS · PRONOMEN

- Personal- und Possessivpronomen
- Reflexivpronomen
- Demonstrativpronomen THIS & THAT
- Fragepronomen WHO / WHICH / WHAT
- Indefinitpronomen SOME & ANY / MUCH & MANY / LITTLE & FEW
- Relativpronomen und Relativsätze
- Die Stützwörter ONE und ONES
- THERE als Vorsubjekt
- Die „beliebtesten" Fehler der Deutschen

❸ VERBS · VERBEN

- Present Simple & Present Progressive
- Past Simple & Past Progressive
- Past Perfect
- Present Perfect Simple & Progressive
- Expressing the Future
- The Passive
- Conditionals / If-Clauses
- Delexical Verbs / Funktionsverben
- Reflexive Verben
- Die „beliebtesten" Fehler der Deutschen

❹ PARTIZIP / GERUND / INFINITIV

- Present & Past Participle als Adjektive
- Partizipien anstelle eines Nebensatzes
- Gerund nach bestimmten Verben
- Gerund nach Verb+Präposition, Adjektiv +Präposition, Substantiv+Präposition
- Gerund nach Präpositionen
- Infinitiv nach bestimmten Verben, Adjektiven und Substantiven
- Infinitiv mit eigenem Sinnsubjekt
- Passivformen: Gerund und Infinitiv

MORE BEAVER BOOKS

GESAMTINHALT und MUSTERSEITEN:
www.beaverbooks.de

ON COURSE GRAMMAR

Unter besonderen Berücksichtigung der Schwierigkeiten deutscher Muttersprachler konzentriert sich **ON COURSE** auf die Präsentation des englischen Verbalsystems.

Einprägsame Illustrationen und variable Übungsangebote ermöglichen den leichten und motivierenden Einstieg ebenso wie den kontinuierlichen Fortgang zu schwierigeren Strukturen und Übungen.

Ein separater 48-seitiger KEY enthält neben den Lösungen ausführliche Kommentare sowie Verbtabellen und eine systematische Darstellung des englischen Verbalsystems.

Format A4; 88 Seiten	**ISBN 3 - 926686 - 14 - 6**
Key: Format A4; 48 Seiten	**ISBN 3 - 926686 - 15 - 4**

BEAVER BOOKS

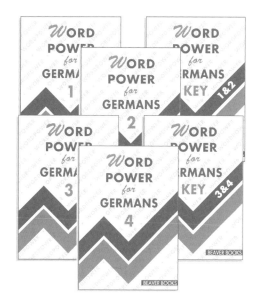

WORDPOWER FOR GERMANS

WORDPOWER FOR GERMANS immunisiert gegen „typisch deutsche" Fehler, macht Stolpersteine bewusst und trainiert die korrekten Ausdrücke mit einer Vielzahl von Übungen.

Band **1 & 2** enthält u.a. ein **A – Z of Difficult Words**: deutsche Wörter mit mehreren separaten englischen Entsprechungen – wie z.B. **Platz** ▸ *place, seat, square*.

Der *Elefant im Porzellanladen* mutiert zum *bull in a china shop*. Neben einer Vielzahl anderer Inhalte präsentieren Band **3 & 4** über 400 solcher deutsch-englischen Idioms.

Jeder Band mit über 80 Illustrationen und Cartoons. Zwei 48-seitige separate KEYS mit Lösungen und Zusatzinfo.

Format A4; Band 1 & 2 sowie 3 & 4 jeweils 64 Seiten

INCREASE YOUR WORDPOWER 1 & 2 & KEY

Ausgewählte Aspekte und Themenfelder des englischen Wortschatzes werden auf unterhaltsame und motivierende Weise präsentiert. Klar aufgebaute Übungseinheiten zur Auffrischung und zum Ausbau der englischen Vokabelkenntnisse. Ein übersichtliches und frisches Layout sorgt für den leichten Einstieg in die Übungen. Separater 48-seitiger **KEY** mit Lösungen, Erläuterungen und zusätzlichem Vokabular.

Format A4; Band 1 & 2 jeweils 64 Seiten; Key 48 Seiten

TARGETS • HOUSE & HOME

Illustrationen und Fotos veranschaulichen das Englisch der alltäglichen Dinge, das mit variationsreichen Übungen und Tests und in seinen metaphorischen und idiomatischen Erweiterungen verfestigt und trainiert wird. Mit 16-seitigem integrierten KEY.

Format A4; 80 Seiten **ISBN 3 - 926686 - 29 - 4**

LOOKING AT LITERATURE

Short Stories, Fabeln, Gedichte und Romanauszüge zur Erarbeitung zentraler – jeweils in Info Boxes präsentierten – literary terms. – **Texte** u.a. von: Mark Twain, James Thurber, Paul Theroux, R. L. Stevenson, H. G. Wells, Edgar Allan Poe, Barbara Cartland, Oscar Wilde, Mickey Spillane, Roald Dahl, R. Pilcher, Pat Conroy.

Format A4; 64 Seiten **ISBN 3 - 926686 - 20 - 0**

TEST YOUR ENGLISH 1 & 2

Zentrale Bereiche des Wortschatzes; reichhaltig illustriert, pro Band 50 unterhaltsame Tests zu u. a. **Spoken English**: treffende Ausdrücke des Alltags • **Compounds**: spezifisch englische Wortbildungen • **Idioms**: typisch englische Redewendungen • **Prepositions** deren Gebrauch vom Deutschen abweicht und besondere Beachtung verdient. Jeder Band jeweils mit integriertem Key.

Format 19 x 24 cm; Band 1 & 2 jeweils 80 Seiten

ASPECTS OF ENGLISH

Germanic Roots • The French Connection • Germlish • English Humour • American English • The World's Language • Standard English, Slang, Dialect • Literary Nonsense & Figurative Language • Advertising English • The Bilingual Debate • Languages in Business

Format A4; 64 Seiten **ISBN 3 - 926686 - 22 - 7**

TOPICS, THEMES & TEXTS

Short Stories, Essays und Romanauszüge, deren thematischer Schwerpunkt zu einer grundsätzlichen Diskussion des Themas geführt wird. – **Topics & Themes**: Honesty • Fun • The Supernatural • Peace for Ireland? • Soap Operas • Genetics • The Short Story • Sexual Equality • How to Write an Essay • Prejudice • Civil Rights Movement

Format A4; 64 Seiten **ISBN 3 - 926686 - 21 - 9**

 KATALOGE, INFORMATION UND DIREKTBESTELLUNGEN BEI

Beaver Books • Marburger Straße 15 • 60487 Frankfurt
Tel. 069 – 77 40 47 • Fax 70 46 35 • www.beaverbooks.de • e-mail: info@beaverbooks.de